ANNA DEACON AND VICKY ALLAN

TAKING THE PLUNGE

The Healing Power of Wild Swimming for Mind, Body & Soul

BLACK & WHITE PUBLISHING

First published 2019
by Black & White Publishing Ltd
Nautical House, 104 Commercial Street, Edinburgh, EH6 6NF

3 5 7 9 10 8 6 4 2   20 21 22 23
Reprinted 2020

ISBN: 978 1 78530 268 8

This book is based in part on interviews about the lives and experiences of its contributors. In some cases names have been changed solely to protect the privacy of others. The authors have stated to the publishers that the contents of these interviews are true and accurate to the best of their knowledge.

Front cover features swimwear by Deakin and Blue, made from recycled plastic found in the ocean.

Some of the safety advice in *Taking the Plunge* is based on RNLI guidelines.
If you are a wild swimmer, you might consider supporting their work: www.rnli.org

A CIP catalogue record for this book is available from the British Library.

Layout by www.creativelink.tv
Printed in India by Replika Press

TO MY BROTHER RICHARD, WHO, THOUGH NOT A WILD
SWIMMER, WAS ALWAYS UP FOR TAKING A PLUNGE.

– V. A.

TO MY GRANNY PAT, WHO DIED THE DAY BEFORE THIS
BOOK WAS PUBLISHED. I WILL ALWAYS BE GRATEFUL
TO YOU FOR TEACHING ME PHOTOGRAPHY, AND
FOR YOUR GUIDING PRESENCE IN MY LIFE.

– A. D.

"I grew up paddling around in peaty brown lochs. And now I love the beauty of the light on the water, the reflections, how it is different every single swim."

ANNA DEACON

"I haven't always been a wild swimmer. But I have a love of the thrill of the cold and a plunge into crashing waves. It was almost a secret pleasure. Not any longer!"

VICKY ALLAN

TAKING THE PLUNGE

ADVICE & DISCLAIMER

WARNING

Wild swimming can be a joy but, like many outdoor activities, it can be hazardous and carries the risk of injury and death. If you choose to wild swim, then it is your responsibility to understand the risks involved and ensure you are familiar with the necessary safety procedures before going in the water. If you're in any doubt, don't swim.

Taking the Plunge isn't a guide to swimming safety and therefore neither the authors nor the publisher can accept any responsibility for damage of any kind, to property or persons, that occurs either directly or indirectly from the use of this book or from any wild swimming activity.

Please carefully read and adhere to the safety guidelines below and take on board the expert advice in chapter 12: Staying safe.

These guidelines are not comprehensive and are for general guidance only. Anyone who goes wild swimming must ensure their own safety.

Before you start:

- **Familiarise yourself with where you are swimming.** Does the situation exceed your swimming ability? Know your limits. Check the tides, weather conditions, lifeguard attendance and whether it is easy to enter and, more importantly, leave the water.
- **Avoid swimming alone.** Especially if you are swimming in remote places, make sure someone else knows where you are at all times, look out for other swimmers, and charge your phone in advance so you can call for help if needed.
- **Never enter the water to save someone else.** Instead, throw them something they can hold on to, and call for help. If there are life buoys where you swim, make sure you know where they are.
- **Never go in the water under the influence of alcohol.** Remember: around half the people who need to be rescued never intended to be in the water.
- **Cold-water shock can kill.** Read more about the effects of cold-water shock and how to manage it in chapter 12.

Emergency numbers

Before going wild swimming, familiarise yourself with the numbers to call in an emergency.

- In the UK, the Royal National Lifeboat Institution (RNLI) is the first point of call for sea safety. If you experience difficulties at sea, call 999 or 112, and ask for the coastguard.
- If you experience difficulties in lochs, rivers or lakes, call 999 or 112, and ask for the police. Please bear in mind that, unlike some beaches and pools, rivers and lakes are most likely not attended by lifeguards.

AT THE START

WHEN TWO STREAMS MEET

THE TIPPING POINT

It began in autumn for both of us – separately, differently, though leading us down the same path across the sands to the Firth of Forth. That was the start, not exactly of the swimming – for we'd both been keen dippers in lochs and seas – but of our adventures in the swim community. It was when we both first got a taste for the regular plunge and became intrigued by what it was doing for us, for our bodies and our minds, the enlivening power of the bracing sea.

The year had been a tough one for Anna, *Taking the Plunge*'s photographer. She had begun to feel burnt out, to find herself exhausted and disillusioned by the weekly grind of commercial shoots, though she couldn't quite explain why. September was when she hit the wall. She was, she says, "Physically, mentally, emotionally wrung-out, utterly spent." It seemed her health was deteriorating day by day. "I was overwhelmed by a feeling of inadequacy. I felt like a terrible mother, letting my kids run wild while I tried to work, taking too many projects on, staying up until the small hours just to keep on top."

In spite of her work backlog, when Anna's cousin, Lil, asked if she fancied a hike and a swim, she "nearly bit her arm off" and took a day off, catching the train, after she'd dropped her kids at school, down the East Lothian coast. Lil and Anna were already regular swim chums, whenever they got the chance, which wasn't often enough. But this time was different – this time Anna had brought her camera with her.

"We arrived at the car park at Tyninghame," she recalls, and from there hiked down to the beach through a beautiful forest, still clinging on to its green in places but starting to lose leaves and take on an autumnal hue. The sky was grey and the air was wet and drizzly, but no wind which is always best for swimming."

What Anna felt, as she got down to that beach, and the two stripped off to plunge into the sea, was that she was beginning to relax. The crashing waves, the cool air and the elements were like a flint, sparking her creativity, and she got out her camera. "I felt a sudden need to capture this moment, this wild place with just the two of us in it. The quiet misty landscape and the wild waves, Bass Rock appearing and disappearing as the haar rolled in. I couldn't stop; everything I looked at inspired me."

The two women ran into the sea. The waves, even in the still air, were huge and bouncy. They stood, thigh deep, staring down the sea and roared. What they cast out into the sea, in those loud roars, was all their frustrations, their stress, their pain and discomfort.

"Is that all you've got?" Anna cried. "I felt the full force of nature," she recalls, "a higher connection, if you like, in that moment. I felt so small and yet so much a part of this earth."

Up above, she saw the geese patterning the sky on their migratory path. On the tideline she watched oystercatchers search for morsels. All the while, she and Lil jumped at and fought the waves. "Like a small child becomes calm after raging, I felt my stress ebb away with the water. I could breathe again, I felt more alive than I had in ages. I let the sea carry off my stress and replace it with huge whoops of joy and elation as our frustrated roars, turned to belly laughs."

AFTER THE STORM

On that day Anna took photographs that were the start of this project, the origins of *Taking the Plunge*. Afterwards, she began more and more to seek out human sea-life, swimmers up and down the coastline, and photograph them. Previously she had documented the sea, now she was documenting the human play within it, and doing so while right in there, wading through the waves with her subjects.

Then Anna began to publish her photographs on Instagram as @wildswimmingphotography. Each time, she asked the swimmers to answer a few questions and give a short biography about why they swam to accompany the images. As the collection grew, that was when she began to notice a pattern. A great many of the people she was shooting seemed to be there not just for exercise or because they loved the water, but because it was helping them cope with or push through something. Some were dealing with pain – fibromyalgia, autoimmune diseases, back pain. Others were battling depression or anxiety. Still others were finding that simply being in the water was helping them deal with some grief or other personal loss.

The answers they gave Anna told a story, one that is increasingly being reflected in current research, about the ways swimming was helping people deal with pain or calm the ever-buzzing voice of anxiety. Anna swam with person after person with such a story. There was Karin, for instance, who came off opiates and

antidepressants once she started swimming. Dawn, who only a few years ago had been unable to walk, but now credited the fact that she was climbing Munros to wild swimming. It seemed as if near-miracles were happening out there in the water.

It was about this time that Anna and I first met. Aptly enough, we were introduced by a friend at an event about the Arctic explorer Isobel Wylie Hutchison. Our friend pulled us together, saying, "Anna, you like wild swimming. Vicky, you like it too. You should get together." What Anna told me then fascinated me – not only the story of her own burnout and pain, and the relief the sea gave her, but also what she was hearing from the people whose photographs she was taking.

MEETING AT THE SEA

I knew the open water as a place of solace myself. I had gone there not in physical pain, but in grief, when three years previously my brother, Richard, had suddenly passed away of a pulmonary embolism. In the fog of that summer, I had found my greatest comfort, my best moments, bobbing around on my back on a lough in Ireland. There I would look up at the pale wash of sky, wondering if Richard were still out there. And, through a friend, also recently bereaved, I'd found myself there again – this time in the sea, joining a group of local swimmers.

I wanted to know more about the swimming experiences of others.

Our first conversation was the start of a journey together. Over six months we travelled across Scotland to meet others who swam in its wild waters. We were there in a bid to find out what they were doing and how it made them feel. The stories they told often echoed each other. There were those who swore by wild swimming as pain relief. Others spoke of the way it stilled their anxious minds. Some described it as a kind of mindfulness.

Soon we were looking into the science behind it all. While the research is still embryonic, it's there and growing – and what became clear was that the anecdotes we were hearing, the personal stories, chimed with medical findings about our cold-water physiology and its possible effects on our mental health. More and more, we started to believe that wild swimming really was good for body, mind and soul. More and more, we wanted to persuade others to try it out, to take the plunge.

But we don't really want people to take the plunge simply because it's "good for you". That's only part of the story. There are many other reasons, each equally bold and good. Because it's thrilling and a lark. Because the sea helps you gain a sense of perspective. Because it connects you to others – from the swimmers of the Hellespont to the hardy "Ice-Milers" to the irresistible urban mermaids. Because, at a time when our human relationship with the planet is so troubled, it's such a nurturing and liberating way of connecting with the environment. Because it's exhilarating. Because, beyond the wild watery landscapes, almost nothing else out there makes us feel so alive.

1

TOE IN THE WATER

HOW TO BEGIN

WHEN THE WATER'S COLD ENOUGH

Even that first toe in can be a challenge.

The first time you plunge into cold water it comes as a shock. Your heart rate rises. You gasp for air. Your blood vessels contract. In fact, if the water's cold enough, you get that sharp, body-quaking reaction every time, no matter how much you might have acclimatised.

Perhaps you are already familiar with it? That feeling, that assault on your skin and your blood vessels, the sharp contraction inwards, the sensation that every cell in your body wants to revolt against what you are putting it through. You know it because you've been there many times before. Perhaps you even sometimes feel like you crave it?

Or perhaps it's something you're only wondering about. You're a newcomer intrigued by the look of crazed exhilaration on the faces of those swimmers down by the shore. They're bonkers, surely, but they look like they're having some kind of wild fun, even if their skin has turned a fluorescent lobster pink. Could it, you wonder, really be that freezing your bahookie off is good for your mind, body and soul?

Well, yes. We believe it can be. We believe, indeed, that there are many excellent reasons to wild swim in the UK, whether in wintry lochs or the more comfortable, though still not entirely balmy, temperatures of early autumn. In our swims across Scotland we've experienced some of these reasons for ourselves. We know, for instance, what it is to have our whirring minds put on pause by the sudden onslaught of cold. Anna knows how it eases her joint pain and banishes her aches. We've heard, first hand, many stories – tales from people who believe their swimming

is a form of self-medication, from others who see it as a form of mindful meditation, or even a route to wider good health.

Taking the Plunge is a sea of voices. All of them, whether swimmer, physician, researcher, athlete or therapist, say a similar thing in different ways. Wave after wave tells a story. Swimming salves. It's good for you. It helps you through.

They also speak of how swimming can take you to places of such extreme natural beauty that all you feel is awe and wonder. You feel small. You glimpse a different perspective on your place in the world.

THE THRILL OF THE CHILL

The temperature is perhaps what puts many people off swimming in the outdoors in the UK. In Scotland, it's the reason our shorelines and lochs are not crowded, but often dramatically and romantically empty. On the west coast, and in the islands, we have some of the most jaw-dropping beaches in the world – long, white sands washed with crystal-clear waters – and all that's stopping most people from plunging in is their fear of the cold. Once you get beyond that and realise that the chill is part of the thrill, and even has heaps of various benefits to offer, a whole world of swimming adventures opens up. You probably don't even have to travel that far to find them.

And it's mostly free. Many people like to start out wearing a wetsuit, or some other neoprene accessories, but really you need nothing more than a bathing costume (and, as some might say, if that) – although booties are nice in winter.

You don't need to be an Olympian or a

supreme aquatic athlete to enjoy the benefits of wild swimming. Many of the people featured in *Taking the Plunge* would be happy to call themselves dippers. There for the quick submersion, they tend to splash around close to the shoreline, rather than go for a long, exhausting crawl out to sea.

The first cold-water swim can be incredibly hard. Perhaps you remember yours – that day you nervously braved the icy waters, and discovered that, after the initial pain, came something else. The world seemed to suddenly open up and you were floating, ecstatic, grinning, marvelling at the fact that you didn't feel just okay, but amazing. Perhaps like Dawn, swim evangelist extraordinaire, you smiled and "buzzed" till the next swim.

Or perhaps you've yet to take that plunge. In which case you might want to heed the advice of Allan, an instructor in the Wim Hof method of cold exposure, who frequently takes people into the waters across Scotland for the first time.

"What I always tell people," he says, "is that when you're learning, set the bar very, very low. Just put your feet in for a while first. If people struggle to get in the sea in the winter, I ask, what are you fearful about? Can you put your feet into the cold? Put them in for ten seconds. There can be that kind of progress to it."

Take encouragement, too, from the fact that (more often than not, we promise), first-timers come out of the water laughing, sometimes shrieking with elation. Alice, founder of the Cairngorm Wild Swimmers group, describes this: "One of the big thrills for me is to see the transformation. Maybe they're quite nervous – and then they come out and there's this huge smile on their face."

A GENTLE INTRODUCTION

You may be wondering what time of year is best to start swimming outdoors. Seasonal sea temperature tends to lag behind air temperature, with water at its warmest – sometimes 14°C off Scotland's coastline – in mid-autumn, and its coolest in March and early April. So, if you want a gentle introduction to the pleasures of wild swimming, it's best to start in late summer or early autumn. Many, once started, keep going right through the winter, as the temperatures plummet, discovering week-by-week that they can still tolerate (and even relish) the chill and that the buzz comes faster.

Even so, wild swimming might not be for everyone. According to Dr Mark Harper, an expert in cold physiology, there are two different body types – the fast coolers and the slow coolers. "If you're a fast cooler," he says, "you just don't like it because you get cold so quickly. Those fast coolers will not reach that enjoyable state many of us slower coolers do. They will just plummet straight down in temperature and their core will become cold."

But, if you have the urge to give it a try, and haven't yet, then one of our biggest recommendations is that you find a local group – there are many of them on social media – and join a bunch of experienced swimmers on a dip. Whether it's the Wild Ones (our local group), Cairngorm Wild Swimmers, Oban Seals, the Wild Highlanders, the Wild West Swimmers or any other group, wild swimming communities tend to be incredibly welcoming and almost always up for coaching a nervous novice on their first entry into the water.

THE JOYS OF WILD SWIMMING

This is a sport that has expanded rapidly over recent years. In less than a decade, Edinburgh swimmers' group the Wild Ones has expanded from tiny beginnings to having over 2,000 Facebook members.

As Jonny Cowie, editor of *Outdoor Swimmer*, a magazine whose subscription figures have grown by 50% since 2017, describes, "When I started swimming outdoors nine years ago, it was definitely considered a bit of a niche pastime – people would look at me as if I was mad if I said I enjoyed swimming outdoors, even in summer. Now cold-water and winter

swimming seems relatively mainstream, in part due to increased media coverage of the benefits of cold water and the continuing growth of outdoor, more endurance-type exercise in general."

But before you start, we strongly advise that you read the safety sections that feature at the back of *Taking the Plunge*. For this is a journey that requires a full health and safety briefing before take-off. Our seas, rivers, lochs and reservoirs are not to be messed with. Hypothermia is real. Cold-water shock does actually claim lives. In 2018, according to the Water Incident Database, 585 people drowned in waters in or off the UK. Seven out of eight of these fatalities were men. However, ninety-three of them were not intending to swim and drowned after they fell in the water.

Yet, much as we want you to keep safe, we also acknowledge that the element of risk is, of course, part of what draws people to the water; it's an undeniable part of its attraction. Wild swimming is all about reaching a little outside your comfort zone, while actually – we very much hope – not getting into real danger. It's about finding the out-of-the-way spots. It's adventure and discovery.

AN ELEMENT OF BRAVERY

For Anna and me, as for many others, wild swimming is partly about the thrill of being brave. It's about finding courage. As Anna puts it, "Even when physically I'm not very strong, going into the water makes me feel mentally strong and like I can take things on. The fact that I am doing this makes me feel brave. And I am brave. It's a mental strength. Mentally, I have

respect for myself. When I've been for a swim, I think, *I've done something amazing today.*"

If there wasn't some little element of fear involved, it wouldn't feel as good, ultimately, as it does. We're not saying this is all about keeping comfortable. Quite the opposite. One of the best tips given by Ross Edgley, the first man to swim non-stop round the entire coastline of Britain, is that, with wild swimming, "You've got to get comfortable with being uncomfortable."

So, go on, take the plunge, venture out of your comfort zone and dip that toe – but please, please read this guide – and the advice in chapter 12: Staying safe at the end of this book – as to how to wild swim safely and considerately first.

WHAT IS THIS *WILD* SWIMMING THING?

Perhaps you're wondering what the difference is between "wild swimming" and the kind of jumping in the sea that so many of us used to do as kids and merely called swimming. Or taking a dip or even going for a splash about. The answer is very little. Wild swimming has become a catch-all description for most outdoor swimming activity in natural waters; it embraces everything from taking a chilly dip in a loch to triathlon training at your local beach, or even competitive open-water swimming at Olympic level. The term

"People have this perception of me going into the sea every day that I must be really strong. But I find the cold really hard, too. The one advantage that I have over those people going for the first time is knowing how amazing it feels afterwards."

ANNA, outdoor facilitator, Edinburgh

was originally coined by the incomparable Roger Deakin, who swam through Britain via its lakes, rivers and seas and wrote 1999's cult classic *Waterlog*. Back then, Roger described his swimming as "wild" because it was done in waters many thought should be avoided for health and safety reasons.

Times have changed. Wild swimming has become almost a craze, and the phrase itself became even more popular after the publication in 2008 of two key books, Kate Rew's *Wild Swim* and Daniel Start's *Wild Swimming*. Some people don't like the term – but it at least makes the whole thing sound like fun.

"I remember my first cold-water swim; I have never smiled so much in my whole entire life. In the photos I'm standing there like Mr Blobby in my wetsuit. But I came out and I buzzed till the next Sunday. I could not wait."
DAWN, wellbeing practitioner, Edinburgh

OUTDOOR SWIMMING SOCIETY CODE

Consideration for others

- Be considerate of your effect on other water users such as fishermen/women, boaters, nesting birds. Be courteous to them and courteous of their rights.
- Be considerate to landowners and properties that neighbour popular swim spots.
- Park sensitively wherever you go: do not block gates to fields or access to houses.
- Properties that neighbour very popular summer swim spots are likely to suffer aggravation. Remain sympathetic and courteous if met with hostility. If there is a way to show thanks or lessen the burden, please take it.
- Take away others' rubbish as well as your own and recycle it. At popular swim spots farmers, landowners and volunteers have to do daily clearance of other people's rubbish: this is not anybody's job, and more hands help.
- Do not scorch the ground with barbecues.
- Be as quiet as possible so as not to spoil the enjoyment of others.
- Keep a good distance from anglers and avoid their lines. Leave them ample room to cast. Pass by quickly and quietly, creating as little disturbance as possible and do not loiter in fishing pools.
- You may want to encourage others to participate. Do not force them.
- Be considerate about skinny-dipping.

www.outdoorswimmingsociety.com

THINGS I NEVER KNEW I DIDN'T NEED

ANNA, Wander Women founder, Edinburgh

My first wild sea swim was on my birthday one September, when the sea is the warmest. My Czech friend, Zuzi, was about to leave the country and she's a swimmer who swam right through the winter. I was just in total awe of her. I wouldn't have stuck my toe into the sea – there was no way. Then she said, "We're going to do this. It's your birthday. Your treat." She handed me a woolly hat – and we went out round the yellow pole and back. The first winter I went every day and went to Portobello's Turkish bath afterwards. But last winter I started to run home in my wet stuff, and what I thought was, "All that equipment – the flip-flops and different towels and shower gel, moisturisers and all these things, a big bag full – I don't need them."

That was one of my main learnings last year. Sea swimming taught me a huge lesson in consumerism. Actually, you've got all you need. You've got the strength. Your body is designed to keep you safe if you listen to its signs. You don't need many things. I personally haven't invested in any swimming gadgets, partly because I'm also terrible at losing stuff. If I bought boots or gloves, I know that one of them would get lost. I thought, "Right I'll stick to the bare minimum and make do with what I've got." That's my little anti-consumerist lesson from the sea.

The best things in life are free – and this is the best example. You're not tied to a timetable or schedule, simply the natural rhythms of the moon and the tide.

STARTING SMALL, DREAMING BIG

ALI, finance lawyer, Edinburgh

If you're just getting started, do it with a good friend you trust, start small, pick a sunny day. Anything to make it less daunting to allow you to get to that point when you're fully "in" – as once you are, there'll be no turning back and you won't need any further persuasion!

HOW TO CHOOSE A "GOOD" SEA SWIMMING SPOT

SARAH WISEMAN, swim coach

Before you go:

1. Aim to swim at a beach that is lifeguarded.
2. Have a look at where other people are swimming. (Ask the locals!)
3. Check the weather forecast and tide timetables.

Upon arrival:

1. Take a while to observe the water. How is the sea behaving?
2. What type of beach is it? Is it sandy, shingles, pebbles, rocky, silty or muddy?
3. Are there any rocks? If so, where? How big are they?
4. Are you in a bay or long shoreline? Is the bay sheltered?

5. Can you see any rip currents? In fact, do you know how to spot a rip current?
6. What is the tide doing? Is the ground wet on a dry day?
7. Is anybody else using the beach? Are there any boat users or creel pots in the water? Are the boats motorised or with sails?

Entry and Exit Points:

1. Plan your exit before you get into the water. Consider any currents; what is the tidal flow and wind direction? Decide how long you are going to be in the sea for.
2. A good choice entry or exit is an area you can get out of quickly if needed. Preferably with not so many pebbles, rocks or much seaweed.

A GUIDE TO TIDES

SARAH WISEMAN, swim coach

Flooding tide

The rising of the sea is known as a flooding tide (tide coming in). High tide is when the tide is fully in.

Ebbing tide

The falling of the sea is known as an ebbing tide (tide going out). When the tide is fully out, this is known as low tide.

Spring tides (full moon, new moon)

On spring tides, high tides are higher and low tides are lower. They occur every two weeks.

Neap tide (first and third quarter moon)

On neap tides, high tides are lower and low tides are higher than they are on a spring, meaning less water moving. These occur every two weeks.

The actual heights and intervals of tides vary depending on location. It's crucial to know the tides of the area you are going to; this information will help you make a more informed choice for a swimming spot!

Slack tides

The hour before and after a high or low tide is known as "slack" tide, this generally means there is less water moving and currents are weaker. But, in some locations, rip currents will be at their strongest. Swimming will usually be easier on a "slack" tide (but not always). An ebbing tide will make it harder to swim back to shore.

What are rip currents?

Rip currents are usually formed when there is a build-up of water on the beach from the tide and waves. They tend to flow from the shoreline back out to sea, and they can take you far out to sea and fast. Rips can also form where estuaries run into the sea. There are three parts to a rip current:

1. The feeder current: Build-up water flows along the shoreline until it finds the easiest path back out to sea.
2. The neck: This is the easiest path for the water to flow back out to sea, could be formed by the shape of the seabed. The current is at its strongest here.
3. The head: Where the build-up water from the shoreline disperses back into the sea.

SARAH WISEMAN'S SWIM SAFETY TIPS

1. Remember to stay safe and tell others where you are going.
2. Where possible, swim with others.
3. Wear a brightly coloured swimming hat.
4. Use a tow float if you have one.
5. Make sure you have plenty of warm clothing for afterwards even in the summer months.

How to identify a rip tide

1. Debris on the surface of the sea is floating away from the shoreline.
2. Sand, seaweed or other items are churning from the seabed.
3. Lack of waves or breaking waves. Waves may break on either side of the channel, but you may not be able to see any waves in the rip current at all.

Rip currents are not "fixed" in place; a rip may change position from one hour to the next.

How to escape a rip

1. Stay calm and conserve your energy. Don't fight with the current.
2. Think clearly. Try and swim adjacent to the shoreline.
3. Once out of the rip current swim directly towards the shoreline.
4. If you cannot swim out of the rip current, calmly float or tread water.
5. If you are struggling, remember to keep calm, face the shore and signal for help by raising one arm.

WHAT RISKS ARE ASSOCIATED WITH WILD SWIMMING?

SARAH WISEMAN, swim coach

Rocks

Rocks can be very slippery when they are wet and can be a potential danger when entering or exiting the water. Be careful with your footwork upon entry. You may want to consider whether you go barefoot or opt to wear some form of sock or water shoe to get into the water. You could also see if there is a more suitable entry point rather than going over the rocks.

Weirs

The purpose of a weir is to deepen the water; they are best avoided. Box weirs are fatal to swimmers who become trapped in them. Do

not be tempted to slide down the face of a weir – the stopper at the bottom creates circulating currents, which will pull you back towards the fall of the water and then underneath.

Jumping and diving

If you want to jump or dive in, then *always* check the depth of the water. There may be underwater obstructions such as rocks and branches. Even if you swim at the same spot regularly, it is wise to check the water depth. Please don't be complacent: if you mess this up, injuries can be life-changing or fatal.

Weeds and reeds

These are usually quite easy to spot, but some may be submerged just under the surface. They are most common in slow-moving warm rivers and some lochs. Where possible try to avoid them: it's easy to get tangled up in them. Try not to thrash your way through them if you do encounter them unexpectedly. Slow your speed down, try and float or turn around slowly and retreat the way you came.

Blue-green algae

This is usually found later in summer months and usually after warm, wet weather. It typically occurs in lowland lochs. A powdery green scum will collect on the downwind side of the loch (the algae bloom). It's very obvious and will feel quite slimy and unpleasant to swim in. Blue-green algae can make you sick and give you a skin rash.

Cercarial Dermatitis (swimmer's itch)

This is an itchy rash that can show up after swimming, usually in freshwater lochs, lakes, marshy or stagnant ponds, though it can on occasion occur in saltwater. It is caused by an allergic reaction to parasites, which usually live on waterfowl and some mammals – the good news is that humans are not very good hosts. The rash is just uncomfortable! The rash and itchiness will usually clear up after a few days, but if you have any concerns visit your local pharmacy or doctor.

Weil's disease

This is the serious form of a bacterial infection called leptospirosis. It's most likely to be picked up entering and exiting freshwater containing contaminated soil or infected urine from wildlife and animals. If you develop flu-like symptoms within one to three weeks of swimming pop to see your doctor. If you have any cuts or abrasions cover them with waterproof dressings, shower soon after swimming in potentially infected water, avoid stagnant water such as canals (in fact, it's generally best not to swim in canals at all), and be more cautious after heavy rains.

Stings and bites

Most stings in the UK are not serious and can be treated with simple first aid, but if you have any concerns, seek medical advice. Depending where you are swimming, the most common causes of stings and bites are from:

- Jellyfish
- Weaver fish
- Sea lice

Cramps

While swimming, cramps usually occur in the calf or foot, when a muscle is tired or overused, dehydrated, or tight from a previous session. Cramps can be uncomfortable and painful, and because they are sudden, they can be dangerous in deep water. If you can, try and exit the water quickly, so you can deal with it.

Cold incapacitation

This can strike even the fittest and most experienced of swimmers. Your body continues to lose heat while swimming (because blood is directed to your core to keep your organs warm). Your arms and legs may start to feel heavy and cumbersome, making swimming very difficult. This is another great reason to swim close to the shore and with other people, so you can exit the water quickly if needed and ask if you need help. To fend off the cold, consider wearing a wetsuit, silicone hat, neoprene hat, neoprene booties and gloves – or any combination of these that suits. (Doubling up on hats is an excellent tip.)

2

CALMING THE MIND'S STORMS

SWIMMING FOR FLOW AND MINDFULNESS

"I struggle to meditate or approach mindfulness in the more traditional ways. The single focus as you enter the water, feel your body react and your mind set free . . . that does work for me."

NIC, lawyer, Edinburgh

BEING IN THE MOMENT

There's no escaping it. When you get into the water, particularly cold water, there's something about that shock to the system that brings you right into that moment, into the present and what is happening, physically, in you and around you. You're there. Alive. Uncomfortable. Aware of everything around you as well as what's going on in your body. The shock makes it almost impossible not to be. The loudest voice in your mind is likely to be the one that is telling you *this is cold*, and, once you've quietened that, suddenly you are there, alive to the world, hearing, seeing, feeling.

Most wild swimmers will talk about this sensation of being in the moment – and when they talk about it, they will often use the word "mindfulness". But you don't have to be a deliberately mindful swimmer to experience this thereness. The bracing cold, the immersion, the all-senses nature of the experience bring you, whether you like it or not, right into the now. Psychotherapist and mindfulness coach, Angie Cameron, has long been encouraging people to find this in swimming.

She observes, "What I think the sea does is make us really feel alive. The sea is there – there's no disputing it. When you're in the water you're not going away off into your head thinking about your work and kids, or whatever else. The experience of the water is right there and, because of that, it creates that mindfulness that comes with being present. We're not thinking about our bills and our shopping, or whatever has caused us hurt or pain."

For Angie, the sea is itself an "anchor" to help us focus in the "here and now". The physical sensations it creates work in the same way as the breath might in other deliberate mindfulness practices. "When the mind stops churning so much," she says, "and we get into our bodies more, we are in touch with the physical sensations. That in itself is mindful. We're using it as an anchor. Every time our thoughts are flitting off to something else, we come back to the swimming or our physical sensations when in the water and this allows us to feel more embodied. If our mind wanders off again, maybe we see something that distracts us or a thought pops up, the sensation of the water keeps bringing us back to the present. So, in that way it's definitely mindful."

These days mindfulness can seem both everywhere – so common that versions of it have been dubbed McMindfulness – and also elusive, and difficult. But mindfulness, as ice swimmer Gilly McArthur points out, is already there in all of us. "We human beings are all mindful, but we just don't realise that we are. So, when you have that first sip of coffee in the morning, for that three seconds you are being present. You're just thinking, 'I'm here and not anywhere else.' Mindfulness is observing the present moment without judgement."

For Gilly, the mindfulness of wild swimming comes to her at the point at which she immerses and is in the water, feeling its coldness, listening to the birds, observing the light on its surface. "You are just there," she says. "You're in that moment without any extra judgement of time and other things. Obviously, it takes practice but the more you do it the more you can just be in that moment."

Gilly has been through her own hard, dark times. In 2012, she lost her daughter, Elsie, when she was stillborn forty-one weeks into her pregnancy. "How you can swim out of that is unthinkable," she says. "What was interesting in that experience, looking back, is how I have a broader understanding that everyone has difficult times in life and that from deep roots into darkness it's possible to grow a more beautiful tree. So now I have, with hindsight, more understanding of hardship and how your mind can, if you set it off in the right direction, grow new buds and new flowers, to make things different."

She and her husband were both rock climbers – a pursuit she took up after she became burnt out in a retail career at Gap. "If you could have cut me in half," she recalls, "I would have been Gap all the way through." In the year after their daughter's death, they decided they would go crack climbing on sandstone pillars in Utah in a bid to do something they loved to help them through the dark times to a happier future. While one hundred feet up one of those rock faces, she fell, hitting a ledge, before being left dangling on her rope with a broken back.

It was while Gilly was recovering that she found a new space to be mindful, and a love of swimming again. "What I really enjoyed about open-water swimming was that it was similar to rock climbing. For me it was an extension of just being in the place, rather than about a measured time and a distance, or monitoring things with a device like a watch. It was always about kicking off my shoes and getting as close to nature as I could. It was about getting away from distraction and calming right down to being in that moment, in that breath."

As the water got colder, towards winter, she discovered "you had to be more in your body" to appreciate the cold. "If you set an attitude when going into cold water that it's cold, it will be. If you go around screaming and yelping, 'Oh my God, it's freezing,' then your mind creates what you tell it to create. If we accept it might be uncomfortable and we are okay with that, that's where the magic happens. That is how our minds work. When you're getting into cold water, you have to be really aware of what your breath is doing and through practice via meditation and breathing techniques, you can calm everything down. It's hugely liberating."

Some people, like Gilly, come to the water with an already developed mindfulness practice. Others find their way to mindfulness through swimming. As Gilly points out, "There are loads of people swimming who I guess didn't have a mindfulness practice, but who are now using it. It's almost like a reversing into a mindfulness practice. I see it as, instead of getting to mindfulness through an app or doing a course, this gives people an experience of how to simply be present. They then might delve further into a course, or into reading about meditation."

FLOWING INTO THE ZONE

But open-water swimming doesn't just take us to mindfulness. It takes us to another state, much discussed by sports psychologists, but not nearly as popularised as mindfulness, called "flow". The term was coined by the psychologist Mihaly Csikszentmihalyi in the 1970s to describe those moments of total absorption in an activity, where self disappears, time abstracts and you are, as some say, "in the zone". Both Angie and Gilly talk about the experience of open-water swimming as one that's not only frequently mindful, but in which we also experience flow.

As Gilly points out, flow isn't the same as mindfulness, though the two are connected.

"Flow state," she says, "is a form of mindfulness in that you're completely absorbed in that moment and you're not thinking about anything else. But it's not the same. In fact, you're so absorbed in that activity that you're not aware of the present moment."

Angie describes the "flow psychology" she frequently experiences while sea swimming as both an absorption and a kind of belonging. "It's not just that you're not thinking about something else, but that you are truly immersed in what you are doing. You are only there, nowhere else, and you feel that sense of belonging. Even fifteen minutes in the sea feels like an hour to me. It's like taking a magnifying glass to each of those minutes, seeing and feeling every little detail."

Like mindfulness, flow is an escape from the noise and distraction that fills our heads. It's about focusing down on one thing, or one activity, which could be almost anything. As Angie describes it, "It's that you become so immersed in the experience you're like a racehorse with blinkers on. When I swim, I'm not thinking about the kids, I'm not thinking about the shopping. The blinkers shut everything out."

ENRICHMENT RIPPLES OUTWARDS

As a rock climber, Gilly has experience of one of the sports that's regularly cited as a typical flow state activity – so she knows well the kind of absorption involved in flow. She has even been a subject in a study on flow in rock climbing led by world-leading research organisation, the Flow Centre.

We can get to a flow state, she explains, when we're doing something that is hard enough to be challenging, but not so hard that it becomes risky. With swimming, Gilly discovered, flow was more likely to happen for her in the winter when it's cold, which is one of the reasons, she believes, she and other cold-water swimmers are more compelled by winter dipping. "That's why I swim way more in the winter when the water is cold. In the summer it doesn't give me the same mental challenge. In the winter the mental challenge hits you into that state. It's hard enough to be rewarding. But it's not so hard that it's totally risky. In the summer it's pleasurable, but there is no mental training going on – not in the same focused way, anyway."

But for many swimmers flow – the word itself can't help but call to mind rivers and currents – doesn't just stop in the water. Research reveals that the more we experience flow, the more we look for it in whatever we are doing. In other words, we can transfer the state we get into in the water into many more areas of our lives. The enrichment can ripple outwards. As Gilly explains, you can find that zone anywhere: "You can train your brain to look for flow."

LITTLE KNOTS IN THE ROCK

GORDON, support worker, Skye

As a support worker I'm quite mentally drained when I finish work. I've got kids at home and I love the kids to bits, but swimming is my way of coming out of the house and just shutting everything down and forgetting everything other than what's in that cave or pool.

I did lots of sports when I was a kid, so I grew up having to do a warm-up, build-up and travel

before activity. So, when I go swimming with my friend Matt, it's all about that whole package, not just the swim. One swim I often think about is one I did at the Falls of Rha. As you're walking there you build yourself up mentally. There's all this build-up in your head, thinking, "No, I don't want to do this." Then you put your feet in and you're thinking, "No, I don't want to do this." Then you go up to your waist, still thinking, "No, I really don't want to do this." And then you're in. Once you're in the water you get that panic feeling coming over you and what I do is I start swimming around and I start looking up. Then suddenly you're seeing what's around you and it starts bringing everything down, and you're starting to take in stuff that you wouldn't otherwise – you're seeing flies buzz past you. It's the whole situation, bringing it down to one tiny little thing that you notice.

There's a set of caves on Skye that I've swam in three or four times. Every time you go in you spot something different. This last time I was taken away by wondering, *Who was last here? How long has this cave been here?* Then I was looking at little knots in the rock. Each time I've been in there I've noticed something slightly different that has taken my attention, and I'll watch it. I focus my mind in on random little tiny things.

WHERE ICE MEETS FLUIDITY

GILLY, ice swimmer and rock climber, the Lake District

My senses are heightened like someone has turned the volume up on all of me. The wind meets my ears, now from the north-west; it's cold, brushing my face and arms. A buzzard cries on a peak somewhere. My heart beats in my throat and then down to my fingertips. My skin hums, a familiar, welcome sensation. It starts in the base of my spine, saunters up my back to the top of my head, and I feel a wave of calm. I breathe deeply, setting my mind, taking that first step.

Cracking with a sound like small twigs snapping, the ice on the shoreline is thin and slippery in places. Placing a definite foot between icy shards and slick, cold rock, I feel the first touch of water. Now I'm connected to this swim. This heady, visceral moment. I push the ice I have cut out of the way as I wade in. I'm aware of its weight; yet amazed too that its hefty mass floats so easily. It's sharp, about an inch or so thick, and milky white. The sounds it makes, dull clinks of glass, and bubbles forming under the ice sheet where my disruption is now sending fresh air under the thick skin of the tarn.

The icy water is now at my waist. I take a deep breath in, and out, and then . . . let go. Breathing out fully to break from my conscious reaction to the cold; pushing against my instinct to breathe in. I focus on my hands moving through the inky water, pushing the sharp ice from my path and, crucially, my neck as I swim. Today the water feels clean, smooth, silky. It can be dense and prickly, but not today.

And I'm swimming. Intentional strokes, my whole body moving, floating over the tarn. Sight engaging where solid ice meets fluidity. There is no judgement here – judgement leads to creeping fear – so it's little more than a gentle awareness of my surroundings. Sensations of cold. I'm smiling, though, so I know this is wonderful, comforting, effortless.

After a while my limbs feel heavier. It begins under my biceps; then my toes start to suffer the cold, right at the tips. I always make sure I have far more time than I need, so I head for shore for the last time to get out and get warm. I'll be back, probably tomorrow, to this deep profound connection to now. Moment upon moment of bliss, joy and calm. My liquid meditation.

JOJO'S MOJO

JOJO, blogger, Edinburgh

The water is an incredible natural mojo injection for me. I absolutely love it for the body, mind and soul. Focusing on breathing is key. I also love to do a body scan, becoming mindful of how different parts feel. I love the way my legs start to feel a burning sensation as my body attempts to heat me up. I also focus on the cold water against my skin and how cleansing it feels. Another option is to focus on your feet and imagine that they are planted into the sand or the rocks, allowing you to feel grounded. Sometimes I like to focus on the feeling of the sun shining on my face or the sound of the birds or the waves.

"You are just here. You're in that moment without any extra judgement of time."

GILLY, ice swimmer, Lake District

A NATURAL HIGH

KIRSTEN, nanny and therapist, Edinburgh

It makes me high. Like, deep down naturally high. It makes me feel like I don't care, that I am just alive. I find it addictive; it fills my soul, which longs to keep reconnecting in a real way. It is also a way to go with the seasons, especially in Scotland. Instead of resisting them, go with them, accept them and love them for all that they bring.

THE HORIZON

ANNE, GIS analyst, Edinburgh

I was talking to my physio – I've been seeing a physio since I had a back injury. She asked me if I meditated, and I said no – and then, I thought,

"Wait, I think swimming must be meditating." It's very mindful. I'm terrible at mindfulness, but in the sea you have no choice but to be aware of your body and what is happening to you. There are always a few moments when I am treading water, looking at the horizon on my own. I guess that's the meditating bit.

MEDITATION IN MOVEMENT

LINDSEY, adventurer and campaigner, ever travelling

Swimming is my way of meditating. A friend of mine meditates an hour in the morning and at the end of the day, but I just couldn't sit down for that long. My meditation comes from movement. Also, water takes you into another world, whereas when you sit down you're still in this world, and I just can't detach.

THERAPEUTIC

SARAH, psychotherapist, Edinburgh

Swimming is part of my own personal therapy. At the very least, it's a mental challenge to overcome, and at its best it's a wonderful form of mindfulness. It can bring you back into yourself.

HOW TO MAKE YOUR SWIMMING MORE MINDFUL
ANGIE CAMERON, mindfulness coach

When you're swimming if you notice your mind drifting off, invite yourself to come back to the present moment by focusing on the sounds around you, your physical sensations, your experience in the water or even your emotions. By doing that you are creating a mindful moment and training the mind. You use the sea, the physical experiences, the breath in the water as your anchor and you come back to that. That's a formal mindful practice and it produces changes in the brain.

WHAT IS FLOW AND HOW CAN I FIND IT?

CAMERON NORSWORTHY, founder of the Flow Centre

People call flow being "in the zone" – and many swimmers will talk of having been there. Cameron describes here what happens in our bodies when we get into that state.

Is wild swimming conducive to finding flow?

Absolutely. It's challenging, which is one of the characteristics of flow activities. It's cold, and there's a huge mental challenge in that. There's a need for the mind and the body to be very congruent and in a state of harmony in order to handle the kind of stress caused by the cold conditions – to allow the blood-flow to go to where it needs to. It's extremely important to not be distracted or to have your attention diverted. Wild swimming would certainly be conducive to finding flow.

How did you become interested in flow?

Flow changed my life. I used to play tennis for England, then I got injured and I got depressed. But one day I met a busker in the streets of Peru who was at a hard time in his life and he was playing like an absolute prince, lost in the music. I was walking by and I was sucked into the music, completely absorbed, as sporting fans are sucked into the game. It suddenly dawned on me that what I missed from tennis wasn't hitting the ball or representing England, but those moments where I'd become so absorbed that I would go to a different place. Since then I've gone on a lifelong pursuit to find flow in everything I do – whether it's parenting, sport or writing.

What happens in our body during flow?

Physiologically there are signs of a great co-herence. There is a congruence between the neuroactivity in our brains and the neural activity happening in the body – which is pretty rare. Everything seems to synchronise physiologically. There's a total focus in one direction, where every part of our mind and body goes "we're going this way" – whether that's electrical signals, brainwave frequency or heart rate coherence.

And what happens in our minds?

In our brains, typically when we're active in our day-to-day lives, brushing our teeth, going to work, there's what you might call a self-aware-ness network at work – but that seems to switch off when we're in flow.

How can we find flow?

Once we find a particular avenue in which to flow – for instance, an athlete might find it in their sport – then we can take those transferra-ble skills and apply them to other areas. Flow feels fantastic. It's like this internal harmony where everything feels like it's meant to be, because everything is pointing in the same direction. It's very satisfying – so the urge to go back and repeat that experience is high. Most people try to find it again in the original activity they found it in. But once they're aware that this state that makes them feel so great is not actually a feature of the rock climbing or the golf or whatever it was that helped them reach it, but was actually linked to their ability to find their flow state, then often they start looking for flow opportunities elsewhere too.

3
BATHING IN NATURE
CONNECTING WITH THE WILD

"Waves keep turning regardless of what is happening in the world, in our lives. Nature is a great comfort and is always there waiting when you seek it out."

MARGARET, photographer

THE INTIMACY OF NATURE

There's something about being in water – the sea, a river, a lake, a pond – that takes being in nature to a whole different level. You are literally immersed in that wildness and it can feel as if you are more connected to the life that bobs, swims and plunges around you than to any other. That same water that runs over your skin runs over theirs too. The sea in which you float connects to waters on other sides of the planet. In it, you feel small, yet also in touch with a vastness beyond yourself. Swimming in the same water as other creatures feels more intimate than breathing the same air. In water, our relationship to nature changes. Away from our own built environments, we are more on a level with other wild creatures, in touch with some other aspect of ourselves.

We know that being in – and within – nature is good for us. The Japanese have been practising "forest bathing" for decades. There's even a word for the connection human beings seek out with other living things – "biophilia", coined by the American biologist Edward Wilson in 1984.

Worcestershire-based NHS psychiatrist Charlotte Marriott has long been interested in how evidence-based lifestyle changes can make a difference to mental health. She notes that the evidence in favour of spending time outdoors, and in particular exercising outdoors, for physical and mental well-being, is "becoming hard to ignore".

She says, "I started to become interested in the power of spending time in nature after noticing the beneficial effects on me and my family. How a long walk in the countryside can defuse an argument, a swim can invigorate and energise, and a stroll through the woods can calm and relax."

Charlotte cites studies that show the physiological and psychological benefits of time spent in nature. "Spending time in a forest once a month," she says, "can increase scores for vigour, reduce scores for anger, depression and anxiety and reduce the risk of psychosocial stress-related diseases." Trees even release chemicals, phytoncides that make us feel better. "They have a direct effect on human immune function and stress hormones."

The list of ways in which time outdoors in nature can help us is long. Charlotte says it has also been shown "to reduce the risk of type II diabetes, cardiovascular disease, high blood pressure, stress, anxiety and depression, and increase sleep duration, perhaps because exposure to green spaces reduces the level of stress hormones: cortisol in saliva and adrenaline and noradrenaline in urine". And, here, in the UK, GPs in Shetland have piloted the social prescribing of rambling and birdwatching.

That sense of biophilia is there in our feelings about open waters. The sea, and other big bodies of water, are wild places. We can't see beneath the surface and we can't breathe, and so we feel like interlopers. Blinded, but for goggles, suffocated but for the gulps we take when we come up for air, we don't know what's down there, what monsters – or other more benign creatures – might lurk. More used to the sea, we might feel panicked by the darkness that greets us when we put our faces into a lake's dense waters, more used to the clear waters of the sea. Yet, curiously, once in these wild waters, many swimmers feel like they belong. They find their wild selves, and they find themselves at home.

"When I'm outdoors is when I'm happy. It was always this thing before of my brain being too active. But when you're outdoors you can turn that switch off."

MATT, swim guide, Skye

A DISSOLVING OF BOUNDARIES

People have always swum in the waters of this planet. Their watery adventures have been recorded in our art; in the paintings, for instance, in the 10,000-year-old "Cave of the Swimmers", with their delightful procession of doggy paddlers. Swimmers are there in mosaics at Pompeii and Ancient Egyptian ceramics. For non-swimming reasons, we have settled next to our seas and waterways, travelled on them, fed ourselves from them. Some suggest we are evolved from aquatic mammals, and there is even talk of us having a "blue mind".

Wallace Nicholls, who wrote a book with that title, in a popular a TEDx talk observed, "When we're with the water, it washes our troubles away. When we're standing at the sea, taking it in quietly it takes away our stress. It's one of the reasons we love the ocean so much. It reduces our anxiety. It connects us to ourselves."

Victoria Whitworth, in her wonderful memoir, *Swimming With Seals*, writes that in the water, "I know I am part of something much bigger than myself. I feel myself dissolving." She relates that feeling to that loss of boundaries described sometimes as oceanic feeling, an idea discussed in the 19th century in letters between Sigmund Freud and the French writer Romain Rolland.

Even looking at images of water relaxes us. Project Soothe, a study at Edinburgh University, has been finding that many of the images we find most relaxing and soothing are those involving water.

For many wild swimmers that sense of connection with nature is one of the biggest reasons they are there. "I was brought up on a farm in the country," says regular Edinburgh swimmer Jane, "and living in a city has always been a bit strange for me, so I've looked for ways of connecting myself to nature and the seasons. I grow veg here. Swimming in the sea feels similar because it's another way of connecting."

ELEMENTAL RHYTHMS

With its tides and swells, its changing currents, the sea is also a reminder that not everything conforms to the kind of timetable we have constructed our lives around. Being in a body of wild water also demands our attention in ways that so much of our contemporary lives don't – it might sound glib, but you can't check your phone out in a loch or worry overly about how Insta-friendly your look is. Wild swimming becomes something of a radical act, a deliberate rejection of digital distractions in favour of more elemental activity. Although online information and specific apps can help you stay safe, there is no doubt about the sea as a vast force beyond human control once you are *in* it. Appreciating that – on a visceral level – truly is a life-changer.

When we're in water, no longer standing on two legs, wildlife seems to notice how different we are too. They regard us humans afresh, eye us in a different manner. Birds study us curiously, as if wondering what exactly we are. Wildlife guide, James McGurk, describes occasions when he has bobbed up close to creatures. "I've swum with a few animals that would otherwise be startled if you approached them on land, but just aren't really bothered about you swimming in the sea."

People, too, seem to have a different take on each other in the water – as if we're all just part of the wildlife. Mary-Jayne is a London-based therapist and eco-psychology pioneer, who swims regularly in the women's pond on Hampstead Heath, which she describes as "a diverse community of women, birds, water and more".

"I'm swimming," she says, "with moorhens, Canada geese, swans and other women. The Women's Pond is the first in a line of ponds fed by a spring. There's a pond for men too, as well as a mixed pond; the other ponds are reserved for wildlife. I don't know anywhere else in the country where you can go and immerse yourself in a wild pond with a group of women; it's a particularly unusual place. Women often come to be quiet, to immerse themselves in nature, so from a spiritual point of view it feels very special."

When we submerge ourselves with marine life, we are reminded of our place in the community that is the ecosphere, and even in history. "Once," says Lil, an East Lothian artist who swims all over Scotland, "when I was getting out of the sea, I saw an otter emerging. I realised I'd been swimming in the same body of water as this beautiful creature. That was really special. We are human, but we humanise our world so much that we claim these environments and forget that they are all part of our planet, and long have been. To be a part of that alongside other creatures who are living there is intensely humbling."

The water humbles us.

That is a common refrain. It puts us in our place, and reminds us of who we are. And we are grateful for that.

GETTING UNDER

LIL, artist, East Lothian

Being in the landscape, in nature, is a key thing about swimming in the sea for me – and it's the one landscape you can get into, right up to your nose. A complete immersion. I was actually scared of swimming under the water after I nearly drowned in Loch Insh when I was about sixteen. I saw an eel and I freaked. I couldn't control my breathing, but someone on a boat saw me and pulled me out. I didn't realise what a fright it had given me until I started trying to swim under again. But last summer, in Orkney,

I finally overcame that fear and I swam under for the first time in years and it was a revelation.

Now, all I want is to get under – that's the real obsession with me. Even without goggles, when you see it all blurred. It's just phenomenal. Talk about getting away from it all. It's another world. There are so many images everywhere now that I think that sense of wonder at new things has been diminished. But in the sea you're discovering a new world for yourself. You're opening your eyes to it, being exposed to it – perhaps just noticing how the sunlight plays on your skin under the water, or how it plays on the rock, or how from above the surface, looking down, a seaweedy place can look really scary and black and uninviting, but if you allow yourself to go underneath you realise that the light is permeating all the way down and illuminating the seaweed . . . and it's a magical world.

It's so reviving and renewing. We tend to get so absorbed in our lives and everything going on in them that it can be hard to get away, but I think the sea is somewhere that doesn't infiltrate. That's particularly so with the winter swimming. It's the hardest, but it's also the most healing – because you really have to be present in that moment. It's about survival and there's not much room for thinking about anything else.

THAT OCEANIC FEELING

BECOMING PEACEFUL

MARGARET, photographer, Loch Ness

Time slows down when you give yourself permission to be still, quiet and to observe. I can sit for hours by water. The very act of sitting and watching is soothing to my soul in so many ways. And in doing so, something magical happens. An ordinary place – a river, a loch, the beach on an ordinary day can turn into a beautiful piece of art. Only by spending time and absorbing the sights and sounds – watching the flow of the water, listening to the beautiful sound of waves turning, watching the light change and the birds fly overhead – do you really begin to feel and see a place. By becoming peaceful and absorbed within that landscape, my inspiration for my photography flows.

AN ESCAPE ROUTE

CHRISTINE, professor of law, Edinburgh

I have always loved the sea. I'd love to live in a house and pull open my curtains and see it. I think the sea is about escape. I've always had two conflicting sides of me. One is very settled and grounded in family and place and commitments and loyalty, and that's definitely a strong part of me, but then I have a part of me that would like to live in a different country every year. I like travelling. I don't feel I need a base. I feel one side must be the true side of me – but

maybe it's not. But the sea is always there *and* always connects you to faraway places, even if you're rooted somewhere. It just always is beautiful.

A lot of the places of conflict I've spent time working in have been on the coast, and actually you see how water is important to people in both good ways and bad ways. The place where this struck me the most was Gaza. I was in Gaza quite a lot in the late 1990s; it's a long thin strip, quite narrow and very militarised. But people are out on little boats and crafts on the sea, and you see women walking in completely veiled, wading with fabric billowing out around them. I often felt like maybe this was a bad thing about it too, that the place was only liveable with its specific conditions because it had the sea there. Even being in such an enclosed space, to see out to sea – and being able to go out and sit in little boats – made it more liveable. There were all sorts of restrictions on people using the sea, and terrible violence happened on the beaches, but the reality is that the sea was there. It's an escape route.

THE DIVING REFLEX

ITAMAR, validation engineer, Edinburgh

I think there is a connection, a prehistorical connection to the water. I studied marine sciences and one of the things we studied was marine physiology and we talked about the diving reflex, which is a reflex that all marine mammals have – and apparently, we humans have it as well. We have a connection to the water. It's just a matter of triggering it. It could be as simple as dipping your head in the cold water.

STAR-STRUCK

NEIL, IT engineer, Cairngorms

Halloween has been my favourite swim so far. There were six or seven of us in Loch Morlich in the pitch dark. It was very windy and you couldn't see the waves hitting you and they would catch you at random. We had tow-floats with glow-sticks attached and some folk had head torches. Then you would have cars coming past and you would just see the headlights for a few seconds and then they would disappear. It was a totally clear sky. Because there was so little light, you could actually see the Milky

Way. At one point I swam out and lay on my back and stared straight up at the sky looking up at its wisps. That was stunning. Wow. Hundreds and thousands of stars. But it was hard because there would be these 18-inch waves randomly smacking you in the face.

THE SKY AND THE SEA

SUSIE, occupational therapist, Edinburgh

I think there's something about the hugeness of it. That's one of the reasons I love the swimming – because you get in touch with the hugeness of things. The sky as well as the sea.

ENCOUNTERS WITH CREATURES OF ANOTHER NATURE

MORAG, retired nurse, Fort William

During my six-hour channel swim from Rhu Point to Eigg, I put my hand on a Minke whale. They were about that day and it was something I'd never felt before. If something touches you under the water, you just scream and kick harder.

NINA, project manager, Cairngorms

A while back when it was warm, there was a toad swimming in the river. I was swimming along and I thought, "Oh no, there's a sheep poo." Then I saw it more clearly: "It's got eyes – oh my God, it's a toad." And it was kind of just looking at me, thinking, "What's that?" as it swam along.

LIL, artist, East Lothian

Torrisdale, early morning. The sea was rolling into the beach in a huge swell, full of seaweed and tumbled stones which scoured our legs as we navigated our way in. Five seals joined us almost immediately. What an amazing swim, the movement of a lively sea carrying us up and pulling us down, almost overwhelming us at times. As we rose to the top of one freezing swell, a seal would be on the top of the very next one, huge eyes watching us intently.

CATHY, B&B manager, Kyle of Lochalsh

Oneroa Bay, Russell, New Zealand. My plan was to swim to the end of the bay and back. Enjoying my swim, I was nearing the end of the bay, heading for some rocks when, on turning my head to breathe, I saw something swimming next to me one or two metres away. I knew it wasn't a dolphin by the shape of its head and by the time my eye was above the water my fears were realised. Just beyond the shape next to me was the biggest dorsal fin I had ever seen in my life. It was an orca, a whopping great big bull. Panic set in and I didn't dare look again as I swam for the shore as quickly as I could. When I got to the shore, I practically ran on water, still not looking back. I saw a couple smiling at me.

I ran to the lady and had a big hug. Five orca – four adults, including a bull, plus a calf – had apparently been "checking me out" for some time. If they had wanted to eat me, they would have done so ages ago, she said. I was assured that it's not known for orca to attack humans in the wild.

CAT, project manager, Edinburgh

One of my favourite swims was when we swam to Fidra island from Yellowcraig and there was a little puffin that landed in front of us. And we were like, "Hello, little one." We managed the swim, landed on Fidra, but then it was a bit like *The Birds* by Hitchcock. We were like, "We better get away."

"Seals are so human-like. There's this one time when I was out swimming and I saw a seal just ahead of me and I swam out to it, and I'd been singing to try to get it to come. There was this moment when I made this really intense eye contact and we just held eye contact for a few moments. I felt high afterwards."

NIKO, artist, Skye

UP CLOSE TO NATURE: THE WILD THINGS WHO SWIM

JAMES MCGURK, Wildlife guide and wild swimmer

The seas, rivers and lochs of Britain are home to a wealth of wildlife you might be lucky enough to see when swimming. Here is a handy guide!

Otters

My favourite has to be the otter. I've seen them fishing in many places I've swum in the Hebrides and the Borders. Remarkably intelligent and adaptable, they can be found all along Scotland's west coast and, thanks to recent efforts to clean up our waterways, in every river system in Britain.

Seals and dolphins

Along the coast, you have a good chance of swimming with seals. Seals can be very inquisitive, often swimming out to investigate human swimmers. I've had seals poke their heads out of the water only a few metres away to watch me and then apparently keep checking up on me throughout my swim.

If you're approached by a seal or dolphin in the water, the best thing to do is relax. They are inquisitive animals and are probably curious about the new creature they've seen. Incidents of aggression to swimmers are very rare. That said, avoid swimming between members of a pod and stay away from their young. If you feel threatened, swim to shore with calm, unhurried movements and the animal is highly unlikely to follow.

Fish and other sea life

Fish often seem to ignore swimmers. I've swum alongside trout in Glen Nevis close enough to see the iridescence of their scales in the sun. Likewise, octopus, crab and other seabed wildlife are easily spotted. If you swim near a seagrass bed, look out for small seahorses and colour-changing cuttlefish. Further out at sea, Scotland's west coast is a major feeding ground for the world's second largest fish: the basking shark, which can reach fourteen metres long. Since they feed on plankton, they are relatively safe, but do not swim closer than five metres. Also, be aware that basking shark prefer to feed in tidal currents, so keep an eye on sea conditions.

Birds

Many birds seem entirely unconcerned by swimmers. Black guillemots are a common sight in shallow coastal waters. You may see these striking black and white birds diving to the seabed to hunt bottom-dwelling fish. Their wings are so well adapted for swimming that they have to use their bright red feet to steer in the air. Out of the water, you may see osprey fly above you when swimming in lochs and rivers, or white-tailed eagles on the coast. The white-tailed eagle's wingspan can reach three metres, making them a stunning sight. Both species became extinct in Britain in the early twentieth century but are now thriving thanks to conservation efforts. Also, shorebirds such as curlew and oystercatcher will often forage near you. In rivers and lochs, the bright blue-green and orange kingfisher is unforgettable. They usually perch in overhanging branches but are most commonly seen as a flash of colour darting along a waterway.

Jellyfish

The only serious threat that Britain's wildlife might pose to swimmers is from certain jellyfish in the summer. The most common jellyfish, the moon jellyfish, has no sting and can even be picked up. It is pale with distinctive purple rings on top. However, the red-brown lion's mane jellyfish has a painful sting. They cannot pursue you and can therefore be easily avoided. Simply stay alert if you notice any jellyfish where you intend to swim. The Portuguese man-of-war (not a jellyfish but a colonial organism called a siphonophore) is very rare here but potentially deadly even if washed up on shore.

LOOK AFTER YOUR ENVIRONMENT

The Outdoor Swimming Society

The joy and adventure of swimming under an open sky is an experience that the OSS loves to share. As a worldwide collective of swimmers, they know how important it is to be actively environmentally aware. Please be a fabulous swimming ambassador and follow this code.

- Protect nature and look after the environment you are using, especially around areas of Sites of Special Scientific Interest.
- Do not disturb wildlife.
- Keep clear of gravel shoals and islands during the spring when birds may be nesting.
- Keep clear of nesting birds, any areas important for fish breeding and spawning and salient otter sites.
- Do not pick up, uproot or trample wild plants and trees.
- Do not remove rocks or wilfully change or disturb land features.
- Be mindful of bankside vegetation.
- Take care not to disturb waterweed and gravel beds.
- Leave no trace. Take all litter with you (including that of others if you can; why not leave a place cleaner than you found it?).
- Do without single use plastics.

THE PLASTIC MENACE

When Karen Bates moved to Wardie Bay in 2014, to a spot near a beach, she was enchanted by her view of "pure sky and sea". However, down there on the sands, she regularly spotted "a mass of distracting litter; anything from a mattress to a child's bike or safety helmet". Right before her she was witnessing, she says, a "measure of the global problem" of human pollution. What, she wondered, could she do about it? Her answer was to beach clean. Here she provides a guide as to how and why to do it.

Why beach clean?

For decades our excessive consumption of junk has been pouring out into the sea, and now the great ocean gyres circulate garbage patches the size of continents. One big question is why we, in Scotland, feel it's acceptable to continue to import fracked gas to feed increased production of plastic right here on our Firth of Forth. Why do we not consider microplastics to be a pollutant and why do we let industry get away with con taminating our beaches with them? By helping to collect the evidence, I feel I can legitimately represent the case for the prosecution.

Organise your own beach clean

People should be positively encouraged to organise beach cleans. It's important to organise properly to mitigate risks, and the camaraderie makes it all worthwhile. Together we can all support each other to achieve much more than we could on our own. It was Catherine Gemmell of the Marine Conservation Society who first showed me how to get started. I went along to one of her MCS beach cleans at Cramond, checked out the resources on their website, and Catherine gave me some kit donated by the council and some names to contact for permissions. I took it from there.

Be aware of risk

Whether you're doing a quick beach clean or a full-blown MCS litter survey, you need to check local tide times and the weather forecast as well as who owns the beach, then assess the risks to the people you want to take part. If you're getting a group together, you're best asking for permission from the landowner. It's important to be aware that if you're picking up sewage-related debris, or plastics, or fishing line and hooks, or even heavy tyres embedded in sand, you can hurt yourself. A sturdy pair of gloves is your friend.

What you might find

Since March 2017, Wardie Bay Beachwatchers have officially recorded 200 bags of junk weighing over half a ton. This massive catch of 42,048 individual litter items consists of a total of 9,463 plastic fragments under 2.5cm, 6,434 wet wipes, 6,275 cotton bud sticks, on average 58% plastic, 31% sewage-related debris and 9% fishing gear. We find agricultural and diabetic syringes, false teeth, plastic toys, razors, toothbrushes, tyres from far afield, and food packaging that's been at sea for decades. On the beach and elsewhere, we've also scooped up a catch of over 180,000 nurdles. Nurdles are the pesky pre-production plastic pellets manufactured at various sites around the Firth of Forth, and brand-new ones keep turning up, particularly at Ferrycraigs beach.

Taking it back to the land

Karen's feelings are echoed by many. The stirring connection with nature that swimming gives us is one that reminds us of our responsibilities. When we swim, we come up against other non-human life and often revel in what we see

there – the birds, the fish, even the unfamiliar tangle of watery plant-life – but we are also, too often, witness to the ways we humans impact on those worlds.

Swimmers often carry that back with them to the shore. Sometimes it moves them to some sort of activism. Sometimes it makes them consider their own daily impact. The surf-activist Nikita Scott – who, as head of the New York chapter of Surfrider has fought both a liquefied natural gas terminal and offshore drilling – once told me she thought it was important for people to find their "moment" that kept them going, helped them carry on in life or keep going with a cause. Hers was floating on her board on the ocean, with a friend, when it started to rain and the drops striking the water looked like diamonds. That was what she called to mind whenever she was flagging. All around her, that sea of diamonds.

4

SWIMMING UP FOR AIR

THE MENTAL WELLBEING EFFECT

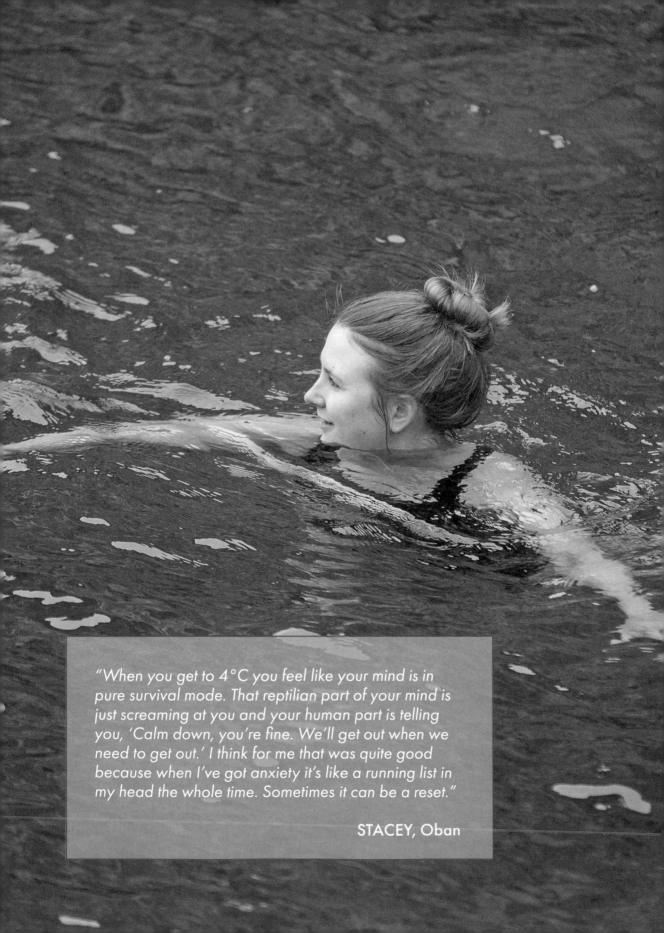

"When you get to 4°C you feel like your mind is in pure survival mode. That reptilian part of your mind is just screaming at you and your human part is telling you, 'Calm down, you're fine. We'll get out when we need to get out.' I think for me that was quite good because when I've got anxiety it's like a running list in my head the whole time. Sometimes it can be a reset."

STACEY, Oban

INSTANT RELIEF

When Anna and I first set out on our *Taking the Plunge* project, we started to hear two things. One was that there were a lot of people out there in the water who were self-medicating their feelings of depression or anxiety through cold-water swimming. We asked a doctor about this and she said maybe the social aspect helped them, or maybe it was something about the water.

The other was coffee-shop talk about the vagus. This is a large nerve that emerges from the base of the skull and wanders about your body, controlling your heart, lungs and gastric system, the kind of bodily functions we tend to think of as relaxation, or as some put it "rest and digest". Over post-swim breakfasts, we would hear speculation about the workings of this nerve. The gossip was that one of the swimmers was trying to get her head under more so she could stimulate the vagus and thereby alleviate her depression. Soon we were all getting our heads down.

There are plenty of swimmers out there who see swimming as some kind of mental-health lifeline. Those, like Matt, a swim tour guide on Skye, who recalls struggling with depression and finding his own way of dealing with it. "That was being outside. I didn't want to do tablets and stuff like that and I figured being outdoors was a big thing for keeping me straight." These days he views being in cold water as a key element in keeping him mentally well. "It's instant relief. Muscle-wise, brain-wise. I always say it's a switch that gets turned on and off."

While research on the mental-health benefits of cold-water immersion or swimming is still relatively embryonic, there's an increasing interest in its potential. One of the people who

has done more than anyone in the UK to popularise the idea that swimming may help those with depression, is the former GP and television presenter, Chris van Tulleken. In one of the episodes of *The Doctor Who Gave Up Drugs* he tested it as a treatment for a 24-year-old-woman who had been diagnosed with major depressive disorder and anxiety since she was seventeen. The results were compelling. Her journey, which included a treatment of six weekly swims, went on to be published as a widely cited case study.

NOTICING THE BUZZ

Mark Harper is the doctor whose research was at the heart of that study. A consultant anaesthetist and long-term wild swimmer, he studied perioperative hypothermia and developed an interest in how a programme of cold water immersions could be used to condition the body to deal better with the stress of surgery. From this, he went on to look at how stimulating the stress response through cold-water swimming might help us deal with stress in other parts of our lives.

As a swimmer, Mark knew that a cold-water dip made him feel good. He'd been aware of that from the very first time he'd ended up in the sea at Brighton after finding his local swimming pool closed. "A friend said to me, 'You should go swimming in the sea.' When he told me they swim all year round, I thought, 'You must be mad.' But I went and swam round the pier and it was 18°C, the warmest time of the year, but I still remember walking up the beach afterwards and thinking, 'Ooh, this feels good.' And so, instead of stopping when the pool reopened two weeks later, I just carried on. For fifteen

years to date. What I now know is every time I go for a swim, no matter how bad I feel when I go into the water, I always feel better when I get out. I notice the buzz."

NOT SO STRESSED OUT

Part of the problem today, Mark says, is that almost all of us experience low-level chronic stress, rather than intermittent big stress. "We used to be worried about running from sabre-toothed tigers, now it's running to get to a train on time. That low-level stress can be reduced. You can do it by adapting to cold water, which means you then cross-adapt to other stress."

As Mark points out, we only have one system to deal with stress – rather than different responses for each stress – and that is controlled by our autonomic nervous system, the control network for our body's unconscious functions. A tight deadline, for instance, triggers an analogous response in that same system as the sight of a sabre-toothed tiger.

"This means that if someone swims in cold water regularly," Mark says, "we can expect them to reduce their response to a different stress – to any stress – like the low-level one of running for the train. In theory, your physiological response to a tight deadline will be lessened because you swim in the sea regularly and are adapted to the stress of immersing yourself in cold water. We're in a constant state of overreaction to small stresses because we don't have big stresses. If we have big stresses, then that reduces our reaction to small stresses. We are designed to be stressed, to just the right amount."

THE HAPPY FIX

But exercising our stress response isn't the only way in which cold-water swimming helps mental health. That vagal nerve our swim friends

talked about is, says Mark, also key to some of the benefits. "When you put your face in cold water, you get this massive parasympathetic stimulation and that reduces inflammation, and that works through the vagal nerve."

The complicated thing about cold-water immersion is that it seems to work on both branches of our unconscious nervous system, the sympathetic (involved in fight or flight) and the vagal-nerve-controlled parasympathetic (in charge of our resting and digesting functions).

As psychiatrist Charlotte Marriott explains, cold water hitting the skin activates our cold receptors, sending electrical impulses to the brain "and this activates the sympathetic nervous system" releasing beta-endorphin and noradrenaline so we feel great, and get a buzz.

But there is, at the same time, the stimulation of the relaxation-promoting vagus nerve that we get when our face is splashed. The activation of both systems in concert, she notes, may help to balance and regulate our nervous system.

One thing that many medical scientists are interested in is the increasing evidence of a link between depression and inflammation, and the ways that cold-water swimming potentially may be of benefit to a whole host of conditions that are rooted in some sort of inflammatory response.

What does this mean for swimmers? How to get your greatest happy fix? Mark Harper says he has never swum in a wetsuit as adding that extra layer means that the cold water doesn't have that same impact in terms of exercising the stress response. "Our response to cold relies on two things. One is the absolute temperature of the water – that's one part of the stress. The other is the rate at which the cold hits your body, the rate at which your skin cools. You don't get that rapid skin cooling in a wetsuit. My thing is I don't mind if I only go in for five minutes, but I want to go in for five minutes in my skin, rather than twenty minutes in a wetsuit. But the advantage of a wetsuit is that you might exercise

more and it's nice to be out in the open water. That's why you wear a wetsuit – and you'll still get all the benefits of vagal stimulation."

APPRECIATING THE WIDER WORLDS

NINA, development planner, Cairngorms

Back in 2017 there was a combination of factors, work-related and home-related that caused me a huge amount of stress. I'd never had depression before, but I'd been with people who had and had been on medication and I understood what the effects of the medication were. I'm a very logical, scientific person and I'd done lots of research, so I knew what I had, but the experience of it took me by surprise. It just seems to be this never-ending gloom. You lose all sense of joy.

I thought I was just exhausted, but then when I was driving one day, a thought popped into my head which was not mine – and was really scary. That was when I knew I had to go to the doctor and get help. I felt that the next step was probably suicide. The doctor was brilliant. But what really freaked me out, and also interested me as a scientist, was that those thoughts are normal. That's what everybody has when they get to that stage. Everybody's brains do that. It's a clinical sign. That was actually reassuring.

The doctor said I needed to socialise a lot more – and because I said I liked swimming,

and I'd heard about the swimming group locally, she encouraged me to go along. At that point I'd rather have stuck pins in my eyes than socialise. Meet new people? I was so exhausted. But I thought I'd give it a try. I also knew being outdoors was beneficial.

I didn't want to speak to the people when I first tried it. But I found you would just swim and by the time you came out you would usually feel better – because you'd had the exercise, and you'd been outside. You'd had the cold-water shock. Then in the coffee room afterwards you could start to engage in conversation. Once it got into winter, it was so cold and so ridiculous that we were all just laughing in hysterics because it was so bonkers. That really helped.

I'm a hell of a lot better than I was. My depression has mostly gone. I was also helped a lot by a life skills course I did, which taught me techniques. But I'm not totally clear. In the winter, over Christmas, it was quite hard and I made a point of swimming. I took part in the national challenge to swim 10km between the start of December and the end of February.

Every day for the two weeks I was off over Christmas, I went swimming. Sometimes I was on my own, so I know it wasn't just the social aspect that was helping. I find just getting in the cold water almost resets you. It helps put things in a bit of perspective. It gives you a bit of time out. Because your focus is so much on how your body is reacting, it really helps to take you away from whatever is causing you the stress. You start to see the scenery and appreciate the wider world rather than just looking at your four walls.

FINDING OUT WHO YOU ARE

LUKE, OSS swim champion

I am a recovered alcoholic and addict. I am also a suicide survivor. But most importantly, today I am a loving partner and father of two boys.

Six years ago, I was a hopeless alcoholic. I used to start drinking from the moment I woke up. I would drink just enough to be able to work and hold out until the end of the day when I could neck a hip flask of Jim Beam on my train ride home and then at home hit the bottle properly where nobody could see me. This had been my "life" for a number of years and I was running out of energy to continue.

On Labor Day weekend 2012, I attempted suicide and am only alive today by chance. My family bundled me off to rehab where I was told that I would be dead in a year if I continued drinking like I did. My liver was packing up and I had early signs of Korsakoff Syndrome. Unfortunately, that was not enough to get me sober.

I spent the next eight months drinking more than I ever had before, pretty much a litre of Jim Beam a night, and sporadically trying in vain to stop. My body was starting to shut down, my hands shook so badly that I could not write or use utensils. My body was so dependent on alcohol that I could not go more than a few hours without severe withdrawals beginning to cripple me.

I was, however, able to have my last drink. And my first day of sober life began on 9th February 2013. The first five days were literally a life-threatening rollercoaster as I went through detox without any assistance (this is

dangerous and not recommended). In the early days, one of the hardest things to do is come to terms with the reality of not ever drinking again. I stumbled here so many times because I was in so much physical and mental pain that the thought of living like this for ever became worse than drinking.

Supported by the AA community, when my sober life began, I made a promise to myself to live my life to the fullest, to illustrate through action that I was a different person. In early sobriety I met the most amazing woman – my partner, Dominique, who has gifted me with two beautiful sons Rafferty and Beau.

Then, in November 2015 I stopped smoking after twenty years. The downside was that I began to crave sweet things – lots of sweet things – and so I started consuming unhealthy amounts of bags of sweets. I gradually gained weight but didn't really notice until December 2015 when I had to go buy "fat pants" as I could no longer fit into my old ones! It was the first rock bottom I had experienced in recovery.

And it was an issue I wanted to tackle. Dominque had always wanted to take part in the famous Lorne Pier To Pub open-water swim. I'd always liked swimming so I thought I could do it too.

We completed my first open-water swim in March 2016 with the 1.2km Half Moon Bay Cerberus Swim Classic and I found that I absolutely loved it. Since then I have completed five (running) marathons and one ultra-marathon, and I now spend every weekend introducing new swimmers to the open water.

I find swimming meditative, especially open water. It allows me to practise mindfulness as I am only ever thinking about what I am doing while I am swimming. I need this respite to

regulate my thoughts and build up the mental strength I need. It has also helped me set and achieve goals, which I believe is critical in keeping me from bouts of depression.

There is something special about swimming in the open water that I can't get in the pool. There is nothing like being in the middle of the bay or ocean. It makes me feel alive. There's also that amazing sense of community and bond of trust you have with the people who you swim with all the time; they look after you and you look after them.

In 2018, I had my first major setback – having to abandon my English Channel swim – and I realised how much swimming was helping my recovery. At that time, I stopped swimming in such an intense way and, slowly but surely, things started to go a bit leftfield for me. I had the worst case of depression I'd had since my recovery began. It was in trying to get back to a "happy place" that I realised swimming was missing from my life and how important it was for me.

Recovery is a supported activity. Never give up. Try everything until you find what works for you to recover. I failed at getting sober so many times it's ridiculous, but you have to work out a way and find a path out. Recovery is never about putting the booze or the drug or whatever down; it's about finding out who you are.

"Lots of things went really badly wrong all at the same time in my personal life and I was looking for a way to manage my stress. Before that period, I was floating along, sort of directionless. Taking up swimming anchored me to something solid. It gave me a code to live by – one that forced me to take better care of myself. I like the shock of the cold water and the way it reboots my brain. The colder and wilder the sea is, the better. It seems to flood me with feel-good chemicals."

GABRIELLA, journalist, Glasgow

SHARING SEA EUPHORIA

LESLEY, artist, East Lothian

I have suffered depression – childhood depression that leaked into adulthood. But wild swimming has helped enormously and it's not just the swimming, it's the people. Oh, it's the community of wild swimmers. They find this instant connection. There's also a lot of creative people doing it. You've got the euphoria from the sea – and then all of a sudden you start sharing ideas.

I do try to swim even when I'm depressed. I know that I need the water. Even if I'm really down, when I come out again, I feel it improves it. I've found that sometimes I don't want to see people and socialising is a struggle. But what happens is that my "shiveries", the folk who

swim with me, they know when I'm like that. It's quite nice, because we can tell one another when we're feeling like that. There's no "I'd better not".

TAKING OTHERS INTO THE SEA

SUSIE, occupational therapist, Edinburgh

I work in mental health and sometimes I feel I would really like it, as a professional, if I were able to take some of the more traumatised adults I work with into the sea. I think it might help them to manage their trauma symptoms. For example, when I first got into the sea in the

winter I was just gasping. My reaction was like a panic attack. And if you gradually become able to manage that when you go straight into the freezing cold sea, you actually grow to be able to manage those really frightening trauma symptoms.

FULL STOP

SARAH, swimming coach and Pilates teacher, Cairngorms

I don't have a particularly busy life as I work primarily part time for myself, but I'd say that I do have a very busy head, which I guess is what anxiety is. I was diagnosed with generalised anxiety about five or six years ago, but I'm quite disassociated from the fact that I have it. So, for me, going into the water clears it all away, and it resets that busyness. It's like a start from scratch, a reset button. I have a busy head. It just never stops.

I like my own company, but swimming is one of the few times I prefer to go with other people, even if it's just one person. It gives me a sort of full stop. There's that pause in the mind on a day-to-day basis. I also think it's amazing how much you can offload in a 30-second swim – the amount of chatting that can go on between you and another person.

When I went along for my first swim, I met loads of crazy people. It was a shock to the system. It was a shock to the system to go into this water, but I also found it quite a bizarre experience. I'd gone swimming with all these people I didn't know.

RAINDROPS BOUNCING OFF MY . . .

CAT, project manager, Edinburgh

I have depression and anxiety sometimes. I have lots of ups and downs, mostly work related, because I'm a project manager and have a lot of responsibilities. Sometimes when it is really bad, I pack the wetsuit, go to Portobello and go in the water. I used to swim in a wetsuit, though this year I started swimming in a costume. The thing I love about a wetsuit is that you can just float. You can lie there and float, doing nothing, for twenty, thirty minutes, looking at the sky. It gives you freedom. I don't think when I'm there – and it's this non-thinking part that is important. It's this amazing thing.

The benefits really kick in during the winter. I find it much more interesting in the winter. For me the winter is the magic – especially when it's snowing, or when it's really cold. It's amazing when it's snowing. You have your eyes nearly closed and see the snowflakes coming in, and when it's raining, I love the raindrops. It's just so comforting. And it's really funny when you swim and the raindrops are bouncing off your bottom, because your wetsuit is so buoyant it makes it float.

I love closing my eyes when I swim – to close my eyes and have a couple of strokes and feel it fully on my body. You feel the water much more on your hands then, the way the water flows around your arms. It's much more intense with your eyes closed.

Doing that stops the anxiety.

There have been times I have been so down I haven't been able to swim. The problem is I overdid it with training for big events. Because of this, for the first time ever I had a complete breakdown. I wasn't enjoying the swimming and my friend, Louise, who I swim with said, "Something is wrong with you, when you don't enjoy your swimming." I was crying in the supermarket. I had panic attacks.

I feel better now because I went to the GP – this was the first time ever I admitted I had a problem – and basically the GP asked, did I need some help. Before that I always tried to manage it with the swimming. But I think I put too much pressure on the swimming, with the events.

I would recommend to everyone not to try the very serious events if you're doing it for your mental health. If you do it for your fitness, go for it. But if you're doing it for your mental health, don't put the events in, because you start training and taking the fun out of it.

Right now, though, I'm feeling so much better. My head has never been so clear before.

THE BUZZ

LIZ, triathlete, Edinburgh

I've always loved the sea but have rarely been bold enough to swim without a wetsuit. I'm a cold-water swimming newbie. I started in November 2018 after reading how it can help with depression, and might help people come off antidepressants. I'm certainly experiencing the short-term benefits: the euphoric buzz is really addictive. I'm hooked.

WALKING INTO THE OCEAN

ANDIE, consultant and copywriter, Edinburgh

I love how getting into the cold water melts away my issues. I've been dealing with a bunch of physical health hassles that have become chronic, which frustrates and worries me on a daily basis. And about two years ago, I developed anxiety. I have ADHD and am well-adjusted, but the anxiety caught me unawares and I still don't know how to deal with it well. Wild swimming helps. It's like I'm shedding all my stress, anxiety and bodily aches the moment I walk into the ocean. I think the acute survival mode that comes with the cold water quiets my constantly running brain. And the exhilaration of it gives me a nice dose of endorphins to boot. It's a temporary relief from feeling broken and, fortunately, it always lasts a while after a swim.

MY ANCHOR

CHRIS, web developer, Portobello

I get quite a lot of depression and going in the water is really important for anchoring me in a way. Going in that cold water cuts through all the buzzing in the head, and the thoughts. It doesn't necessarily make me feel great but it makes me come back to my head, come back to my body, come back to just being me.

THE HEART SOARS

NIAMH, carer, East Lothian

I'm autistic and a very big part of swimming for me is a sensory thing. I feel euphoric in cold water. It's a deeply satisfying, tingling, fizzy feeling that leaves me feeling powerful, grounded and connected to nature. I feel awkward on land and awkward in social situations. In the water, I feel my body is doing what it is meant to do.

I was diagnosed as autistic as an adult. I think I became aware of it when I was about seven or eight, but I didn't have a word for it. I knew that there was something that I had to hide and it was confusing. My son is now sixteen; he was six when he was diagnosed. I didn't recognise anything for a long time. When he did things, I would just think, "But I do that." Even when he was diagnosed, whenever experts said anything, I kept saying, "But I do that." But it still didn't sink in properly because I had such strong preconceptions about autism and, to me, it was something that affected boys and was more of a children's thing. I was pregnant with my second son when I was diagnosed and he's diagnosed now as well.

I swam with my dad when I was tiny, and he was really into outdoor swimming. He used to go to Gladhouse reservoir regularly for a swim and sometimes I'd go with him – but he often went on his own too. We swam outdoors wherever possible. Then, I didn't do it for ages. As a teenager you lose touch with a lot of the things that you used to love and after a while you come back to them. But we lost my dad in 2011 and I used going for a swim as a way of remembering him. He died in late March and

I went for a swim in the sea on the first anniversary of his death. I'd never swum in water that cold before and it felt wonderful and I suddenly realised *I love doing this*. At first, I fitted it into any sort of anniversary or connection to my dad and then it became more and more. The beauty of finding the local group was that it became easier, because I don't really like to swim without somebody keeping an eye on me.

Swimming can be a solution for the issues around autism. But I think everyone has to find their own solution. One of the things that I often get is this untethered feeling, as if something is loose. It comes from excitement sometimes. But it's not always a very pleasant feeling. It's a feeling that I need something. Really intense exercise or swimming helps.

The other great thing about swimming is the peace. You're just getting the noise of the water. And you can escape chatter. The experience is the only thing that's there in my head. My heart soars. Extreme joy.

I don't think there's one thing at the heart of autism. In my family it's really strongly linked to hypermobility. As a biologist I think there is a link between extreme hypermobility and autism. It's a biological issue for us with something to do with connective tissue. There's something genetic about connective tissue disorders.

There's a lot more research going on into autism and what's called interoception now. It's your internal awareness – the connections and feedback signals within your body. That makes a lot of sense to me. We don't always notice when we're hungry. Or we have a slightly different connection. If I'm hungry, I'll think, "There's something wrong. I don't feel good. Could it be hunger? Well, these are the signs of hunger . . . do I have those?" Tired, hungry, thirsty – all these things have to be rationalised and logically thought through. It's exhausting, the amount of thinking through everything.

I have to be careful with the coldness when I swim – many autistic people do. I love the coldness and it creates a greater euphoria for me, but I'm not very good at temperature regulation and knowing when I'm too cold. I've come close a few times to being pre-hypothermic and I do sometimes just crash where I need to sleep for a day or so afterwards. So, I definitely don't feel the same thing that other people say – that it cures everything and makes them feel better. Actually, it's something I have to be really careful about with my health. I'm much more cautious now than I used to be, because I want to keep doing it.

TO DIP OR NOT TO DIP? SELF-CARE WHEN WILD SWIMMING

KATE SWAINE, nutritional therapist and long-distance swimmer

Open-water swimming is a wonderful activity with so many benefits for the body and soul, but, as with any physical activity, we have to look after ourselves.

If you're new to open-water swimming you are unlikely to have as much "tolerance" of the cold as those who've been doing it for months or even years. Even an extra minute or two in the water can be the difference from warming up relatively quickly and painlessly when you get out or remaining cold and shivering for way longer than you might have expected.

The vast amounts of energy the body uses to warm you up when you're really cold can leave you feeling exhausted for the rest of the day. If you are someone who suffers from low energy, this is something to pay attention to as, instead of the swim being energising, it could turn out to be just the opposite.

We are bombarded with the claim that exercise improves energy and helps your immune system – and it's true that, generally speaking, exercise, including open-water swimming, is a vital part of feeling energetic and having healthy immunity. However, there are times when we need to go gently with our bodies – and cold-water immersion doesn't always facilitate this. If you feel you have a cold or virus coming on, then being cold is a challenge to your immune system. You aren't going to catch colds from being cold, but viruses spread very quickly in the cold, and if your body is using tons of energy to warm you up afterwards then that energy can't be directed to your immune system. Cold-water dips are good for our immune system when we are well, but if we're run down, then it might be wise to stay out of the water for a while.

The key is to listen to your body: if you feel great after your swim, with a spring in your step and the ability to get on with your day effectively, then that's how it should be. However, if you feel more lethargic than usual or struggle to get through a workday, post-swim, then heed that and take it easy for a while.

"I started wild swimming last summer. Friends with mental health problems had been egging me on to try it for ages, but my hand was somewhat forced by the fact I'd signed a contract to write a book that included a whole chapter on the benefits of cold-water swimming for mentally ill people. I have PTSD after a series of extremely traumatic events. I've been ill for two and a half years, and I've gradually been adding outdoor activities to help with my recovery. Swimming has become one of the essentials. The swim itself helps me feel removed from my troubles. It's a multi-sensory experience that brings me back to the present and out of the torture chamber in my head."

ISABEL, political journalist, London

5

OUT OF OUR DEPTHS

GETTING IN TOUCH WITH DISCOMFORT

ROMANCING THE COLD

In midwinter, as the temperatures plummet towards zero, there are swimmers who choose to ditch their wetsuits, worn over the summer for endurance training, in favour of bathing suits. They do it for the love of cold – because they want to feel it in all its intensity. Cold, for them is a romance. When the temperatures rise in spring, extraordinary as this may seem, they fret. Their beloved cold, and all that it gives them, is leaving.

Among these winter lovers is Alice, known as "Alice the Hammer" because of her habit of driving around with a large sledgehammer, which she uses when she wants to crack a hole in the ice on one of her local Cairngorm lochs.

"I've always been fairly good with the cold," she says. "The difference is that I now feel addicted to it. I get excited by the thought of getting in that cold water. Then that completely

goes away for a few minutes and I'm actually getting in it and I'm like, 'Oh my God, what am I doing this for?' Nowadays I get a 'I really need to get in' kind of feeling. That's new. Because I never used to be dying to get into the ice."

These days, we humans have got good at surrounding ourselves with creature comforts. The environments we've created, at least in the developed world, mostly revolve around them – heated car seats, air-conditioned malls, duvet jackets, hand warmers, rooms that are neither too hot nor too cold, comfort food.

THE OPPOSITE OF COMFORTABLE

But cold-water swimming is the opposite of comfortable. People who wild swim will often talk of getting out of their comfort zone, or – different, though similar – feeling vulnerable. They may feel this for many reasons. Because of the cold, or because they are bobbing on the surface of a liquid that has the potential to drown them, or because of childhood fears of monsters from the deep. Just as some swimmers fear but also love the cold, others are terrified by the ocean's depths, but still swim out over them.

Research has shown us that some of this stress – this vulnerability – can be health-enhancing. It's good for us to find those moments when we feel a bit out of our depths. We can learn to appreciate them. Swimmers will often describe their thrill at the cold-water shock. "I think it is addictive," Alice says, "and it's also beneficial, mentally and physically."

Stacey, a swimmer with the Oban Seals, describes her favourite moment when it's cold as "getting in". She says, "I know a lot of people hate it, but I love the getting in, and if it's really cold I might try to get in by myself, so I can really spend time thinking about what I'm feeling, because it is quite extreme."

MEET THE ICE MAN

Few have done more to popularise the idea that getting out of our comfort zone in the extreme cold is good for us, even healing, than Wim Hof, who is known as the Ice Man. Using his own invented breathing and training system, Hof has climbed up Everest and Kilimanjaro in nothing but his shorts and shoes, and he holds twenty-six Guinness World Records, including one for swimming under ice. He even seems to be able to control his own immune system. The claims Hof makes about his method seem outrageous – that it can help counter autoimmune disease, arthritis, depression, autism – but he is developing an ever-increasing following. Whatever it is Hof has, plenty of people want it.

His phenomenal endurance has, unsurprisingly, drawn scientific attention. As yet there's not enough evidence to prove that his method produces all its vaunted benefits, but there is growing interest in the research field of cold exposure. Wim himself has been a lab rat, his body and brain tested by, among others, researchers in the United States, who found that he was able to activate an internal pain-killer function in his brain during his response to cold-water immersion.

One of Hof's messages is that modern life isn't good for us – for our brains or our bodies. In our comfortable, heated, air-conditioned worlds we are "de-stimulated". We are not exposed to the kind of environment for which our physiology is built.

Most swimmers don't come to cold-water

swimming – or find appreciation of it – because of Wim Hof, but many have come across his ideas. Anna Neubert-Wood who runs WanderWomen, a series of events which revolve around being immersed in nature, recalls the impact of reading *What Doesn't Kill Us*, a book about Hof in which the journalist Scott Carney tells the story of how he went on a Wim Hof retreat to debunk him and became a follower.

"Wim Hof," Anna says, "talks about environmental conditioning. He says that in our forefathers' generation, humankind was so much more exposed to the elements and that the body is designed to deal with a lot more than we give it credit for. One of his arguments is that the body still wants to fight something, but we don't give it the chance to fight the cold or the hot. So, the body made up illnesses like anxiety, like depression, like allergies and immune diseases. I absolutely think that must be true. These do all seem to be modern illnesses and I'm sure it's got something to do with the fact that we don't expose ourselves to the elements any more."

INTO THE NON-COMFORT ZONE

The Wim Hof Method is partly spread through certified instructors, such as Allan Brownlie, who runs courses, workshops and retreats in Scotland and further afield.

"I always tell people," he says, "that you have the comfort zone, and then you have the non-comfort zone. Then if you really push it further you go into that danger zone. Sometimes when you have a good understanding of what the cold can do to you, it is good to go into the danger zone. I've done that."

Allan believes that this "non-comfort zone" is important. "When something gets uncomfortable you learn something. You learn that pain is only temporary. You can relate that to anything. Being uncomfortable emotionally is a bit painful. The non-comfort zone is probably at certain stages the learning zone, where you progress. What you want is definitely not always to be in the comfort zone. If you're in the comfort zone all day, if you do that all the time, it's very boring, for a start."

Three years ago, he recalls, he was living another, quite different, life, one which he recalls led him to develop anxiety and lose weight, dropping to around sixty kilos. "It was so many things together, and that emotion just sent me over the edge."

The phrase Allan uses to sum up this time is that he was "too much in the comfort zone". He was working as a sales rep for a nice company and "not coming out of my comfort zone, in my job or my relationship, starting to accept things". As he recalls, "I wasn't taking risks, I was focused on somebody else rather than being focused on me." He describes this phase as his "other life", his "previous life" – the one before Hof.

One of the first things that strikes you about Allan, after you've got over the piercing pale blue of his eyes, is that he seems, unlike many of us, unrushed. He's perfectly on time – yet he seems unbothered by time. "What I discovered through the Wim Hof, when I discovered my breath," he says, "was that time doesn't matter – it's all about the progress, the meaning and improving myself. Time doesn't matter with that. It just feels so freeing."

Through his Wim Hof courses, Allan has introduced many people to cold-water immersion. "When you're in cold water," he says, "people think about their extremities quite a bit – their hands and their feet – because all the blood vessels are just closing up and trying to protect the vital organs. But they shouldn't think of it as a fearful thing. It's a natural thing."

He believes we evolved to submerge our hands and feet in cold water, as we fished and foraged in the shallows with our hands. "Our hands would have had to work in cold water. That's what they were supposed to do. The reason you feel the pain in them is that the blood vessels close off too sharply. They should close off in a smooth way, in a quick way – but what you're feeling is the pain because they're not used to working like that."

THE HABIT OF COURAGE

Of course, you don't need the Wim Hof Method to be able to get into cold water. Most people do so without the help of his breathing strategies and have found their own way of tackling it. What they all share, however, is a knowledge of what it's like to face feeling uncomfortable.

This zone of discomfort, that space where we're perhaps not in danger but aware of some risk, is something that ice swimmer Gilly McArthur mentions. She talks about "peering over edges" into the dark spaces that we're scared of – both physically, and in our emotional lives. "It's about having a mindset in which you know if you do some particular thing then you will push your comfort zone to become just a wee bit bigger."

Gilly knows the dark places – she broke her back during a rock-climbing accident and lost her daughter, who was stillborn. But, she says, all of us have those edges, those places.

Some psychologists believe courage is a habit, and the more we practise it the easier it gets. In our swim travels we often heard stories of how the bravery found in the water was giving people confidence, that it was spilling over into other parts of their lives. A ripple effect happens. Their hearts grow braver on land, too.

Lil is one such swimmer. An artist living with fibromyalgia, she says swimming has given her a boost. "Somehow the restrictions of my illness don't matter any more, because I realise I can live really fully despite them, and I know that I can still push myself into spaces that are for me, like climbing Everest. It has made me more courageous. I've started working in a way that is maybe more risk-taking, because I have confidence in that. I am now running art courses which I had been scared to do, but they have been really successful. I think, 'If I can get in the sea in February, I can do this.'"

SWIMMING THROUGH FEAR: A GUIDE

HELEN DAVIS, sport psychologist

The cold, the jellyfish, the depth, the dark. There are so many unknowns in open-water swimming. What if you have to get out and can't manage the cold? What if you get freaked out by a big fish? The depth can frighten people a lot – particularly if they are to be going any great distance. I take a personalised approach and select psychological techniques depending on who I'm working with to support each individual client. Here are a few.

1. Visualisation

This can be very effective, but you have to learn how to do it and do it well – commit to practising it by doing it on a regular basis. There is a lot of evidence to suggest how effective it can be. I take my clients through the techniques for doing this by making it as realistic as possible, by including details such as sounds and smells. It can be used for a whole array of different things; for example, visualising the mass start of a swim, coping with the cold or keeping your stroke technique when fatigued.

2. Self-talk

Listen to your inner monologue. I work with quite a few Channel swimmers and areas of concern could be swimming into something – perhaps a jellyfish. There is a lot of uncertainty with Channel swimming, and you don't know till you get in what you're going to come across. With a jellyfish you can prepare for how you will react if it happens – but generally unknowns and uncertainties can raise anxiety. The discussions I have with swimmers talk about how those threats are still going to be there, so it's a question of how you manage them. I work with clients on how they can use their personal resources to help themselves manage threats.

Keep calm and breathe, or float, on

There are things that can make you panic. A bump on the head or something like that could derail you in the moment. A lot of people just when they're getting in the cold find their breathing takes a while to establish. I teach

relaxation techniques, such as ratio breathing. Here you inhale for four, hold for two, exhale for six or seven counts. Just to bring the heart rate down. But some people like to just roll on their back and look at the sky, just distract themselves from how they're feeling. Floating is always a good strategy if you need to take a moment or two to resettle.

Have an emergency plan

If something scary happens, what are you going to do? I work to help clients psychologically prepare as much as they can by planning. This planning might include a "go-to" place, a place you have planned for, that gives you a course of action in the event of something untoward happening. It's a psychological safety thing. This might happen to you, but if you know your "go-to" plan well and can remember it – it can help you in the event of something scary

happening; for instance, an actual encounter with a stinging jellyfish or being knocked by someone in a mass swim.

WHATEVER NEXT?

JACKY, former occupational therapist and pet shop owner, Callander

I've always had bad vision. I've only got 2% now, but I maximise what I've got. I had my right eye removed two years ago, just because I couldn't see out of it and the pain was too bad. But I was wanting to find something that I could do for myself – but while having people around me.

Pool swimming was boring, just going up and down and up and down and I knew I liked the outdoors because I did scuba diving many years ago – and I wanted to overcome my fear of open water, of deep water and dark water – and I decided to push myself. I'd been trying for years to find something.

The first thing my wife Jane knew was when I went, "Ooh look what I got in the post!" and it was my swimming wetsuit.

She was like, "Whatever next."

I can see the definition between the hill and the sky, but I can't make out detail. I can see that the water is there because I can see the light on the water – but I can't see the detail in it. I can't make out that much detail, but once I know where I am, I sort of get used to it, but I still need some guidance at times.

It does look different every time I come down. And what's really lovely is that in the different seasons, you've got over the hill, the auburns. I can make out the colours, but I can't see the things like the contours.

If someone said, "Look at that tree over there," I would be, "What tree?"

Swimming is that zen moment. It's your zen. Swimming gives you peace. It gives you a sense of wellbeing. And, we're mad – you've got to be a bit of a nutter to get in there. For me it's not distance, it's just the water, it's nature. We've got so much of it here in Scotland and it's beautiful.

I still haven't overcome my fear of the dark water. It's funny, because I know I can swim, it doesn't worry me so much. But I still think, "That's really deep. That's really dark." I don't particularly like that. There's also the seaweedy aspect. As soon as that wraps itself round my ankles, it freaks me out.

Floating on your back is nice, and I sometimes float face down and everyone thinks, "Oh my God, she's having a diabetic seizure."

I'm just enjoying the breathing out and seeing a few bubbles.

Once you've got over that initial cold, you can lie on your back and the water just moves you – you're not having to do anything. It's kind of a nurturing experience. If you're lying back, you can hear the water and what's happening underneath, but you're part of it.

With the swimming, I can be just me. Once I'd got over my fear of the actual swimming, because it took me years to learn to swim properly, I found that going out there, knowing there are other people there, I could be myself. I have Dawn who swims alongside me and makes sure I'm aware of where we are – because I do tend to zigzag. My friends will be saying, "This way, Jacky." They enable me to have that freedom but keep an eye out for me.

I was diagnosed with diabetes last year and I've not been that well and so it has curtailed how often I can go in the water. But Jane set up this pool in our back garden. It means I can go out there, get my strokes in. I've got a belt on and I'm tethered to the decking. It's a lot cheaper than buying an infinity pool.

Whenever family or friends ask, "Why do you do that?" I say, "Because I can. Because I want to. Because I love it. But also that it's mine. It's everyone else's if they choose it – but it's my little bit of freedom."

A long time ago I learned to scuba-dive, to get over my fear of water. Never did, but it enabled me to do something and know that I could breathe. I used to rock climb and abseil because I was scared of heights. That wasn't about getting rid of the fear, but about owning what I can do. It doesn't mean I've overcome my fears. I still am scared of heights.

What I'm doing, when people put you in this

bracket as having your limitations, is saying, "Nah. I can achieve things." But I need to push myself. Jane encourages me. She says, "In you go."

Swimming has opened up a new world. It's introduced me to people. You can have a communication with someone you're never going to meet, halfway round the world and they can say, "Oh, we've been swimming in the Pacific and it's 28°C," and I'm like, "Come to Scotland." Or when we go to Norway next year I've said I'm going to swim in the fjords. I also plan to swim in Nepal – going in two years' time.

For me swimming is pleasure. For me it's just getting in the water. That's my pleasure – and that's my distance, isn't it? I'm not a runner. I would need to be on a tandem for a bike. I've done the London Marathon and I've done the Edinburgh MoonWalk and I'm not doing them

again. You've got to find the one thing that makes you want to do it again and again and again. And I want to still be doing that when I'm eighty, if I live that long.

AN EPIC LUNCHTIME

ALICE, founder of SwimWild, Cairngorms

You don't have to go in for very long with an ice swim, that's the thing. You go in for a short amount of time and you've got that buzz. I always think it's like, say, summitting a Munro in that you get that amazing view and incredible sensation of *Wow! I've done it*, but with ice swimming you only have to go in for thirty seconds – so I can do it in my lunch break and

get back and feel like I've done something really epic. Yet all I've done is smash a hole in some ice, had a dunk and got out again, warmed up by a fire, drunk a hot chocolate and back to work again.

When you go in the ice you have to be careful not to get cuts or bruises because you don't feel it so much. Either the chunks of ice are bashing against you, or if they're really thin slivers of ice, they can also be cutting. So, it's just about being really careful. I definitely would put on socks and gloves as well, because if you're going to be touching any ice then it can be sharp.

It's an escape. My life is pretty busy and I think the intensity of the cold really helps because it's so intense you can't think about anything else, so you really get into the moment. Whatever else is going on in your life it's just a moment that is yours.

TALKING TO MYSELF

MATT, swim guide, Skye

For me swimming is always about pushing my boundaries. I generally go through a bit of an argument with myself in my head. Recently I did a swim in a loch that's at 600 metres on the Cuillin Ridge. It took me five hours to walk, pitch my tent, and then the day after it's about a four-hour walk up on to the ridge for a swim. I didn't know the route up, so I was finding my own way – and there were a couple of parts where you were climbing. I'm having this discussion with myself, telling myself, "This is probably a bit risky. Should turn around." Then arguing with myself, saying, "No, you're fine,

you're fine." They're my favourite swims where I'm pushing myself. Then you get up to the loch and you go, "Shall I just head back?" Then you have literally a conversation in your head, convincing yourself. Of course, I've come all this way, so there's no way I'm turning back, but I do quite enjoy having that conversation with myself because it's me pushing my boundaries. If you're not having that conversation, you've probably not pushed yourself.

INVIGORATION

ROSS, part-time dog walker, East Lothian

I've had a fear of deep dark water since I got trapped in a covered swimming pool when I was younger. Now I find I love waves and

big swells and lying on my back watching the sky. I feel relaxed and invigorated at the same time, nothing else matters when you're out there. I completed the Firth of Forth crossing in September 2018. That was exciting as it was my first real swim in open water. In 2019 I did a night swim at Portobello; the water and the sky were that inky black colour which I had feared for all those years. I loved it.

OVERSTAYING YOUR WELCOME

ITAMAR, validation engineer, Edinburgh

You learn your limits as you go along. I think one of the times I was learning about my limits we went to Threipmuir, a beautiful reservoir with lovely views and cows and sheep around. It was a winter swim with a big group. We all parked the car and went in the water and the water was just below 3°C. I overstayed. Everyone was coming in and out and I was like, "It's fine. I can't feel my fingers and toes but I'm used to that. Usually when you lose sensation, it comes back!"

It's vasoconstriction; the body protects the core. It shuts down the extremities and brings the blood to the centre, keeping the heart and lungs, everything that's important, warm. But when you come out of the water the blood rushes back out and you start feeling your fingers again, and you feel warm because your warm blood actually comes out to your skin. And it can be snowing outside and you're just standing out there all warm and nice – but you're actually starting to have hypothermia by this time, so you shouldn't stay too long.

On that occasion I noticed that half an hour after coming out of the water and everything, I still couldn't feel my fingertips. I thought, "This is weird," and it took me about two months to regain full sensation in my fingertips.

HYPOTHERMIA AND HOW TO TREAT IT

DR CLARE EGLIN, lecturer in physiology and expert in cold-water response, the University of Portsmouth

Here's a checklist of what you need to look out for if you're worried that someone in your wild swimming group is becoming hypothermic.

1. The signs

The individual will feel cold to the touch and usually they will be shivering violently and will be very miserable. They may show behavioural changes like aggression or introversion and they may have slurred speech. They may be clumsy and become confused.

2. What you should do

The first thing is to stop the person from cooling any further. Remove them from the water, insulate them and shelter them from the wind and prevent any further evaporation.

Exactly what you do will depend on the situation – how cold they are, the environmental conditions and the facilities available. So, ideally, take them out the water, remove any wet clothes, dry them and get them dressed in lots of dry clothes (including a warm hat). Then take them inside or into a warm car to keep them out of the wind and so you can monitor them closely.

If inside isn't an option, cover them with something windproof – a survival bag is best but a strong plastic bag or waterproof clothing will also do. This will stop cooling due to

evaporation and wind. If they are mildly hypothermic and fully conscious, a warm sweet drink and getting them to move (walk) will increase their rewarming rate and is usually more comfortable than just shivering. Please don't leave them on their own or let them drive a car until fully rewarmed.

If you have one available (I admit this is unlikely) a hypothermic person can be given a warm bath (at about 38°C to start, increasing to 40°C when it can be tolerated – test water temperature with your elbow as with a baby's bath). The warm bath is the fastest way to rewarm a hypothermic individual, but be careful when removing them from the warm water as they may feel dizzy.

Seek emergency medical attention if symptoms are severe. Call 999 to request an ambulance.

"I'm having this discussion with myself, telling myself, 'This is probably a bit risky. I should turn around.' Then arguing with myself, saying, 'No, you're fine, you're fine.'"

MATT, swim guide, Skye

WHAT IS AFTERDROP? AND CAN I TAKE A HOT SHOWER?

MARK HARPER, official medical adviser for the Outdoor Swimming Society

Most people are susceptible to afterdrop. You go in and you swim around, you get out and you're feeling fine, but then it hits you that you're really cold. Don't try to solve it with a hot shower, though. People collapse in the shower because they have a really hot shower afterwards, and that opens the blood vessels up to your skin and then all that cold from your peripheries heads back into your core and makes it shockingly cold again.

ARE BODIES OF FRESH WATER COLDER THAN OTHER BODIES OF WATER?

SARAH WISEMAN, swim coach

In short: no. They aren't usually colder than any other body of water; however, larger bodies of water do behave differently to smaller bodies of water.

In the spring and summer months, the surface layer in lochs will begin to warm. This is due to the rise in both air temperature and radiation from the sun. Warm water is less dense than cold water and will float. This top surface layer can be anything from one metre deep to twenty (potentially deeper in larger bodies of water). Water at the bottom (or in the depths) of a loch

will be much colder, potentially as low as 4°C. There is a narrow thermal layer in between the surface layer and the bottom layer called a thermocline. In this layer the water temperature drops rapidly!

In summer, it is worth knowing about the thermocline layer, especially when you are jumping or diving into the water. You may well encounter much colder water far more quickly than you were expecting.

"I love being immersed, literally, in nature, the buzz from the cold water, the community and camaraderie of fellow swimmers. I always think when one of us talks with passion about the joy of swimming in open water, our enthusiasm rather than actual words will be enough to encourage others to try it."
DEBBIE, swim teacher, Edinburgh

6

BEYOND THE BREAKERS

ADVENTURES BIG AND SMALL

"Adventuring makes me feel alive. I generally dislike cities, dislike repetition and dislike sitting indoors when I could be outside."

CALUM, swim adventurer

THE TRIBES OF WILD SWIMMING

Within wild swimming there are many tribes. There are the taut, impeccably muscled, wet-suited triathletes, the competitive types, the "skins" swimmers wearing nothing but cossies, the social dippers there partly for the cocoa and chat, the ice-breakers, the lone seals. But whichever tribe you belong to, if you're wild swimming, mostly it's likely you're there for the adventure. You're there for the thrill that you get when you discover a new pool or have to pull up at the side of the road because the loch looks irresistible or when you walk down to your local bay and discover the sky is a glorious ice-cream pink.

The swim adventure is not a new thing. It has a long history – some of it bound up in huge, unthinkable swims. When Ross Edgley decided to swim around the entire coast of Great Britain in 2018, one of his inspirations was Captain Matthew Webb, the first man to swim the Channel in 1875, who did it in spite of the fact that it was widely believed to be unswimmable and others thought he was mad. He even did it in a heads-up breaststroke all the way, since any other stroke was considered "ungentlemanly".

NOT FORGETTING: GERTRUDE ERDELE

The English Channel remains one of the world's great swim challenges, and since Webb, over 1,800 people have completed it. In 1926, at the age of nineteen, Gertrude Erdele became, on her second attempt, the first woman (and sixth person, beating the previous record by over two hours) to do so. Gertrude died in 2003 at the age of ninety-eight, having spent her remarkable life teaching deaf children to swim.

And in September 2019, in a "superhuman" feat of endurance, American cancer survivor Sarah Thomas became the first person to swim the Channel four times non-stop – she swam an extraordinary 215km in 54 hours.

ADVENTURES ON A SMALLER SCALE

But for many the adventure is smaller. Their Channels are less time-consuming, more local, and doable on an evening or afternoon off. Perhaps their adventure isn't about a goal or a distance, but about discovery and having a laugh with a friend. They are on what the writer Alastair Humphreys would call a

micro-adventure – small trips that anyone can do, ideally from their front door and with little specialist equipment.

Humphreys came up with the concept to democratise adventure, to save it from the tough, ex-SAS professionals and rich guys. He wanted it to be accessible to us all. And wild swimming fits neatly into that category.

All you need is a swimming costume – if that – and a patch of wild water, and in Scotland where we live, for the most part, no one can stop you from diving in, or charge you for it. Of course, you can swim the Channel, the Corryvreckan or the Bosporus if you want, and many do. But you can also find adventure as an occasional dipper.

THE OCCASIONAL ADVENTURE

"Micro-adventures are great," says Outdoor Swimming Society ambassador, Alex Sehgal. "I was first introduced to this concept not too long ago, but it's been a game changer. Life can get stressful and monotonous so having a short trip or activity planned gives me something to look forward to. For me micro-adventures help keep things fresh and serve as a motivation to get all my work done so I can go out and play. I get bored easily so having these outings little and often keeps me engaged. They're also a good way to de-stress and forget about work."

Alex explains that one of the virtues of a micro-adventure is that it really could be anything. It's not a means of travel, but almost an attitude. "I find the term micro-adventure quite ambiguous, but that's half the fun. The only real essential is a can-do attitude."

Regardless of location, equipment or transport, you can micro-adventure. For instance, Alex doesn't have a car, which makes the planning, particularly when she's heading to remote places, more complex. "A bike," she says, "can help massively. Take your two-wheeled steed on a train or ferry and then ride on from there. It definitely makes the adventure more exciting . . . and helps justify the cake and coffee stops."

For many swimmers the ultimate micro-adventure is a swim safari, the multiple-stop-off day or weekend tour of new and unusual locations. Swimmers talk about a four- or five-swimsuit day, and have systems for managing their changes, which often include putting on a dry swimsuit underneath their clothes after each dip in preparation for the next.

TOP OF THE WATER TEMPERATURE CHARTS

Among the most high-profile of swim adventurers in Scotland is Calum Maclean. whose Gaelic television series *Dhan Uisge* and vlogs of remote plunges have made him something of a wild swimming celebrity. He's probably most famous since his Scottish water temperature chart vlog – in which, instead of referring to temperature in degrees, he talks about the water as Baltic or Hoora cold or Roasting – went viral.

Calum says his favourite thing is to find new and unusual places. "I have quite an inquisitive mind when it comes to the question of: Could I do that? And that question makes me keep seeking out new adventures and new places. I want to see more of Scotland, I want to find places I've never been to, I want to be overawed by the sensation you get from swimming in a stunning place. I want that excitement, and I want it regularly."

But among his more cautionary tales is one of a dip that he took on Skye. Calum recalls that it was a chilly December day and he decided to take a short drive and go for a swim in Loch nan Dùbhrachan in Steat, a body of water in which, so the mythology goes, a kelpie resides. The loch is right at the side of the road and has the advantage of being easy to get to. "It was just one of those days," he says. "You had the urge, you had to go for a swim. I didn't quite realise at the time how cold it was."

The water, he remembers, was extremely cold and dark – "intimidating", in fact – but still he had a really nice swim. When he got out, however, he was really cold. "And when you're really cold," he says, "you get tunnel vision, where you can only focus on one thing – so putting your socks on becomes really important to the detriment of actually putting the rest of your clothes on."

He managed, nevertheless, to get into his clothes, jump in the car and put the heating on, before deciding to head back home. "I started driving," he says, "and I'd probably been driving for about thirty seconds and there was this big lorry coming towards me and the lorry was on the wrong side of the road. It was getting closer, and I was really confused because I could only focus on just being there. The lorry was coming nearer and nearer and the driver started flashing the lights and beeping the horn at me."

The truck was within about fifty feet of Calum's car when he suddenly realised what was going on. "I was driving on the right-hand side of the road. I didn't realise because I had cold-water brain. I pulled over to my own side. He drove past and he was flashing." For Calum, it was a serious lesson. "I learned from it, big-style. I never drive now with that kind of cold-water brain."

THE SWIM SPOTS OF SKYE

Calum is one of many who have made the seeking out of new swim spots a way of life. On Skye, for instance, Matt Rhodes is a tour guide who believes he now knows the waterways of the island better than anyone. There are days, when he's working as a swim guide, in which he does five or six swims a day – in waterfalls, healing pools, the sea – and others when he's on his own, or with swim pals, and goes about finding a new remote pool.

"I know places," Matt says, "that take five hours to get to. There's a place I want to take the guys to and you've got to walk up a stream for about five hours and there are five or six pools all the way up. You walk up and you're like no one would come up here – because there's just no reason to go there except to explore. They didn't have time to explore fifty or a hundred years ago because they were working so hard, working the land. You would only go somewhere like that if you had lost a sheep or something."

SWIMMING BIG

These micro-adventures, however appealing, are not enough for everyone. Some people are more about the big goal – about setting their sights on something and training for it. These are the people for whom adventure is as much about battling with their own bodies and inner resources, as discovering new locations. They know what it takes to stay out there and keep going. A strong competitive urge is perhaps present, too, for these swimmers.

The stories of those who strike out for those big goals, and what it takes to conquer them, has been covered in many a book and film, and it's something we only touch on here – save to say that they are an inspiration. They show us what's possible, where you can get to when you swim off from the shore, way beyond the breakers.

CALUM'S TIP: When considering all these things, kayakers and their guidebooks are often a great source of knowledge. If you can speak to a kayaker who is also a swimmer then that's the best, as they will have a clear understanding of what can be done.

THE CALUM MACLEAN GUIDE TO SWIM ADVENTURE

1. Making a plan

Depending on where I'm going, I'll do lots or very little research. I'll often ask someone else for their opinion – but at times I've been told "you can't swim there", then done it anyway without any issue or concern.

I'll always use maps, look at the weather and consult kayaking guidebooks. If I'm going alone, I'll let someone know where I'm going and when I'm due back. Ideally, I'll have someone with me, but this isn't always the case. I like the challenge of being alone.

When it comes to the sea I always try and seek local advice if it's an unknown or unusual area. The sea has caught me out on occasion; it is such a powerful force and commands our respect.

2. Find new places

I am a map geek and, being a hillwalker, have always enjoyed discovering new places. In some ways, finding the outliers is interesting: the highest loch or the deepest. But there's way more to an adventure than ticking off some gung-ho list of (ever more ridiculous) extremes. A place that is visually or aurally interesting always grabs my attention. I like somewhere that feels wild, somewhere far from the drone of cars. I'll always ask locals, and often a casual comment can lead to a seed being planted. An old story, the Gaelic meaning behind the name of a loch, a tale from bygone days . . . all these offer fascinating ways to think about new locations.

3. Be safe when adventuring

In my opinion, knowing your own ability and any specific risks that a location might present are key to keeping you safe. It's vital that you think about and understand questions such as:

- How long can you swim for?
- How long can you stay in cold water?
- How do you react to being held under by a wave?

Judging your own abilities is something that comes over time. It's a case of building up fitness, knowledge and comfort in potentially uncomfortable conditions. The importance of this can't be overstated. The more you challenge yourself, the more you can withstand, and the more you start to understand what kit is needed, and what isn't.

Think beyond yourself, too. Look at the specific risks of the location.

- What is the water like?
- If it's the sea – Is there a current? Boats? Rip tides?
- Is it somewhere I can look after myself, or will I need a safety support?
- The main question to ask is: where can I get in, and where can I get out?

And the answer to that last question might be that sometimes I won't get out where I planned – but as long as I can get out somewhere and make my way back, then I'm satisfied! On the other hand, I've sometimes walked several hours through snow to reach a swim and then decided against it when I've got there as it just didn't feel right. It's no big deal – the water isn't going anywhere!

"I think it is a mental thing. I think you really have to be quite mentally strong. When I swam the channel it all went well for seven hours and then I got told: They don't think you're going to make it."

MORAG, long-distance swimmer

"Adventure to me is not about reaching the highest summits, walking the furthest or reaching certain physical goals, to me it's more about the journey. The journey inwards, it's about connections with like-minded people, connections to nature that surrounds us: one doesn't have to go very far to experience adventure. Finding your own path and owning it is what it's about."

ANNA, outdoor facilitator

YOUR MICRO-ADVENTURE

ALEX SEHGAL

Sometimes micro-adventures require intense planning to get the most out of the short time you have available; others happen on the fly. They can be as simple as an activity right on your doorstep or an impromptu overnight away. Living in Scotland, it helps to check the forecast . . . although, that being said, I would suggest preparing for all weathers and always taking a waterproof with you, no matter the weather report! It's good to know what sorts of elements you'll be up against e.g. winds, tides, temperatures – particularly, of course, with actives involving water.

Sunshine always makes the world a brighter place, but as the saying goes, "There's no such thing as bad weather, only bad clothes!"

Alex's micro-adventure kit list

- Rucksack (a classic 25-litre is perfect)
- Waterproof jacket
- Hoodie and other clean dry warm clothes
- Hat or beanie, and gloves
- Map and compass or equivalent technology so you don't get lost
- Water bottle
- Flask with boiled water (or prepared hot beverage of choice)
- Collapsible lunch box and cutlery set
- Microfibre towel
- Dry bag (to keep stuff dry!)
- Granola bars or flapjacks
- Strawberry laces (they're GREAT for energy AND entertainment)
- Hand sanitiser
- Lighter
- For overnight trips, add in sleeping bag and bivvy/tent
- And don't forget your cossie if you're planning to swim in one!

BEGINNER ADVENTURES

EMMA, mother, Edinburgh

Swimming has brought me so many adventures. It has been life changing. I've done it for recovery and to have a life of my own when my children are away overnight at their dad's. Adventuring gives me a real high, improved stamina and energy: an incredible sense of achievement. It started small with getting in at Portobello during jellyfish season. Now I'm climbing hills, wild camping, kayaking and smashing ice to swim in freezing water. My confidence is growing. I feel like my life has started over. A second chance. I'd advise anyone thinking about it to just do it. Find like-minded people – join a club, brave social media – if you're not confident enough to do it alone. Build up to it. Baby steps.

SUPER-SWIMMER TIPS FOR A BIG SWIM

COLIN MACLEOD, swim adventure guide, Isle of Lewis

I recently swam across the Big Minch Channel, from Gairloch (on the Scottish mainland) to Lemreway (Isle of Lewis), a total distance of 33 land miles in 21 hours and 1 minute to raise funds for Cancer Research UK, my total for which has now reached over £8,500.

Over the years I've built up the distances I can swim in open water, starting from half a mile, as I like to keep challenging myself for the next one. Last year I promised my mum that I would do a swim for Cancer Research UK as she is a local committee member. So, I swam the 15-mile Little Minch Channel from the Isle of Skye to Harris and then thought *what next?* I realised I could raise more money by swimming the Big Minch Channel.

This was actually my second attempt; I had to stop the first time. I felt very frustrated (to say the least!), as the finish was less than a mile away. It was the first time I hadn't organised a swim like this for myself so I was disappointed in the lack of sea support. What I learned was that if I'm not 100% happy with the level of safety cover then I won't be doing the swim.

People sometimes ask how I manage to keep going. To be honest, the way I think I can do it is by being able to compartmentalise and get on with the task at hand. Also, I enjoy my surroundings, everything I see around me I find really fascinating. I tend to play a wee game; it's like word association but with songs.

If you're thinking about doing a big swim, I would suggest you train for the event by gradually building up the distance that you're going to be taking part in. This enables you to figure out what works for you mentally and what you have to do to achieve your goal. Also test your feeding regime, trying to replicate the event itself. Someone once told me that you can swim in a day what you can swim in a week. You don't have to do the distance in training, but you do have to be confident in your stamina mental and physical.

SWIMMING THE ENGLISH CHANNEL

MORAG, retired nurse, Fort William

I think it is a mental thing. I think you really have to be quite mentally strong. When I swam the English Channel it all went well for seven hours and then I got told: They don't think you're going to make it. Because I was getting swept west, just with the tide [a common problem for Channel swimmers], so I wasn't really moving forward very much. I was just devastated. All these things were going through my head. I was thinking I don't want my admiralty chart and I don't want any photos. Then I thought I'm just going to keep swimming and see what happens and actually for four hours it was touch and go. It would have been so easy to say all right, take me into the boat now. But I didn't.

My husband would say I'm stubborn. I don't like to give up. Just achieving each bigger distance gives you the confidence. Swimming Windermere was a big turning point for me – the fact that I swam it and enjoyed it. On the whole I'm quite a positive person. I broke my arm the year before I was supposed to swim

the Channel and that was really devastating. I remember seeing a surgeon who said, "You'll never be able to swim front or back crawl again." He said that raising my arm to about shoulder height would be the best I could do, and that if I wanted to swim the Channel it would have to be breaststroke. That was a bit dispiriting.

But I managed to train myself up – and it was just determination, being really good at doing my physio and going into the swimming pool and doing my exercises in there. At the beginning, I would put my hand up to open a cupboard door and it would get stuck there – I would have to put the other hand up to physically lift it down.

I used to be the most awful coward at getting into the water. If we went swimming as a family, they would all be in and out the water quickly and I would still be standing up to my knees chittering and not going in – but I find it really easy to throw myself in now. That happened about four or five years ago. I went swimming with somebody who just went in and it helped me to just go in. That's been quite a transformation – and it's how I set off on the Channel swim: I just went in.

NIGHT-TIME AT LOCH LOMOND

ALICE, swim events organiser, Cairngorms

When I swam the 39km of Loch Lomond the water temperature was okay, but the night-time air temperature dropped down to about 4°C. So that was the really hard thing. By the end I felt cold. But a lot of it is in your head and you have to keep talking to yourself. The thing that I kept telling myself was: I can cope with this water temperature. This water temperature isn't actually any colder than I'm used to swimming in.

SWIMMING WITH EFFICIENCY

MAX, research scientist in physical oceanography, Oban

Swimming is time in my own head. There is very little noise underwater to distract you. I can concentrate on the weight of the water on my hands and forearms, not rushing and losing grip, how the water feels as I rotate and glide through it and on doing it better next stroke – like a very satisfying optimisation process, trying to be most efficient. In open water you also have currents and waves that change your stroke and swimming on the Scottish west coast provides plenty of opportunities to explore, both above and below the crystal-clear water. These can be rocky headlands, sandy beaches or castles to circumnavigate.

7

SALT
TEARS

SWIMMING
THROUGH GRIEF

"Out on the loch, I would lie on my back staring at the big sky, wondering where in that vast wash of cloud, I might find my brother."

VICKY, writer, Edinburgh

WHAT COMES TO THE SURFACE

When you're out there on the water and start talking about what matters you realise that the sea is a place where a lot of people come with their loss. Griefs float up on the swells. Names bob in with the tide. Conversations come around to a friend or lover or sister or brother or mother or father, no longer with us, yet somehow brought to mind. One swimmer, told us how, following her mum's death, a friend suggested they go swimming, saying, "Your tears will mingle with the saltwater."

Some people make their first wadings into the water to find comfort, or release; others, swimmers already, find their regular practice is what helps them through. There are many reasons for this. One is that, as Angie Cameron notes, the sea can be very like grief itself.

WAVES OF GRIEF

"I think," she says, "the waves are like grief. Sometimes our grief is like a big tsunami wave, sometimes little waves, sometimes we are calm and sometimes it's like we are being taken along with the swell of the water. If we're genuinely going through grief, whether it be a normal grief, or a trauma grief, it's like the sea, with its waves – they come and go in their strength and intensity. There's something so predictably unpredictable about the sea and that's not too dissimilar to grief. It's a simple parallel."

Sometimes grief comes at you from nowhere. Sometimes you can be feeling fine and calm, then you notice the waves building from a distance, as if your whole body was some

stirring ocean, volatile and meteorological in nature. Other times the waves will be suddenly there, engulfing you, throwing you down on to the bruising, abrasive sand, salt in your eyes, water-choked.

Angie observes that she has come across quite a lot of swimmers who talk about loss and grief, but not all grief is the same. She points out that trauma grief isn't the same as general grief – and, while swimmers tend to talk less about trauma, it's definitely something she believes they bring to the sea.

She herself has experienced both types of grief – the sort when, fourteen years ago, her brother died after a car accident left him in a coma, and the full body-blow of trauma grief when her sister committed suicide, and when one of her children was stillborn. Angie recalls that, following the loss of her sister, there were times when she was "metaphorically in a cave without even a match lit".

Angie sometimes takes people, struggling with not just grief but also depression and anxiety, into the sea. "It's not something that I openly advertise," she says, "but if people have lost their way, they've reached a place where they're not able to find meaning in their life – I find to go into the elements of the sea can have a profound effect and bring us back to life."

"Quite a few of my physiotherapy clients who have experienced depression and anxiety," she says, "have come off their medication as they have found their time in the sea is so healing."

OUR LIVES AGAIN

What, she thinks the sea does is make us feel more alive. It helps us, in the face of death and loss, find our own way back to life. "If," she says, "there's one thing that death teaches us it's

that you've really got to make the most of your life and take it by two hands. I remember when my brother died, I said, 'I promise you I will never take life for granted again, because you don't have the choice.'"

The sea also provides a space in which we, in some metaphorical yet physical way, can swim through and up. Like grief, the sea feels overwhelming, a huge force against which we are tiny, powerless. Yet we can swim, we can float, we can let our bodies tumble through the waves and then kick up. We can surface. The water is a place where we take risks and push ourselves, all the kind of things that actually, when we're grieving, Angie observes, we tend to stop.

BUOYANCY AIDS

Many swimmers talk of the healing power of floating within grief. Itamar, for instance, who swam through multiple, successive bereavements – his father, his brother his aunt, his grandmother – says, "There is something about flotation, this floating in the water, this looking at the sky, where you don't hear anything, and there's no disruptions, particularly in a loch where it's so still. It is a kind of a stress reliever. Floating there, and thinking of everything, your mind very clear. Absolutely no disruptions."

Itamar was struck by the power of floating on a visit he made to some flotation pools in the Red Sea in his home country of Israel. He's even tried to reconstruct the process of guided supported flotation in his local swimming pool. Any kind of floating, he says, works well for him. "I've done it in Gladhouse reservoir. I always try to just float. Floating, no gravity,

no nothing, breath, some clarity. And together with the temperature of the water, it's like all the worries of the week and what's coming next week, dissolve. You don't feel anything. You just enjoy the moment."

Angie echoes his love of floating. "When I'm floating," she says, "I'm allowing myself to be vulnerable and exposed. I think death, or grief, actually gives us that too. It gives us that depth of openness. Anything could happen in that float. But yet if we can meet that vulnerability with this aliveness, within the rest of the world, then that's pretty bloody awesome."

AN ACT OF TRUST

That feeling of trust and openness, when we float, is something many swimmers identify. As Bryony, who recently lost her mother to cancer, describes it: "I remember my grandpa teaching me to float, when I was little and we lived in Kenya. I couldn't do it for ages, because it's quite scary putting your head so far back. He would put his hand on my back and say, "I'm here, I'm here." You have to really put your head back in the water. Maybe there's something about trusting there; you're trusting the sea to hold you up."

AN OCEAN OF CONNECTIONS

But many come to the water for some spiritual comfort – or at least arrive with a kind of magical thinking. The sea or lochs, like the sky, seem to be a space in which we see connections, particularly while we are in the full onslaught of grief. Shapes in the clouds seem to speak to us.

Birds seem to carry messages. Knox recalls that in the first few months after her mother died of pancreatic cancer, she saw and felt connections all over the place, especially while in the sea.

"I felt she was trying to say things to me. Once, when I was lying on my back and I was thinking of her, I opened my eyes and I saw this perfect arrow of birds just flying straight over." Now, she says, she sees those signs less. "Maybe it shows my grief has changed and lessened, that I'm not looking for those signs as much. I don't need them as much."

The sea is so vast it seems to connect with everything – including our departed loved ones. Frequently, while floating, we have some sense of being at one with the universe. It's no wonder that those of us who have lost go there in the hope of finding something, or someone. It's no wonder we find comfort there.

A WATER BOY

ITAMAR, validation engineer, Edinburgh

I was always a kind of water boy. I grew up in a kibbutz in Israel and we had a swimming pool. In the kibbutz everything is free and shared. After school you go to work in the fields and after that you go to the swimming pool and spend hours diving and swimming. I've never actually learned how to swim properly. My grandfather threw me in the kibbutz pool and it was like either drown or start swimming. I think I copied what I saw on television, the Olympic swimmers.

I spent many hours and days there. There were these high boards that you could jump from and try to somersault. Later I went to this semi-military boarding school, where we learned naval skills and after that I went to study marine sciences. I was always close to the sea. But that was a different sea from the one here in Scotland, a little bit warmer. The coldest it gets in the Mediterranean, on the Israel side, is about 16°C, in February to March, and over here that's pretty much the hottest it gets in the summer.

My first swimming experience here was when I gave myself the challenge of swimming in Loch Lomond, the Great Scottish Swim. I just signed up. My brother had a brain tumour and I was raising money for brain tumour research. At the event they have a section where you acclimatise to the water. I thought, *Yeah, I can handle cold water. Come on? How cold can it be?* Then I got in, and I thought, *Oh my God, this is so cold.*

When I started swimming, I already knew about my brother's illness – he was diagnosed in 2012, at the age of twenty-eight, with a brain tumour of the type that is usually benign, but turned out to contain some cancerous cells. When they realised it was actually a more serious tumour they operated. There was a two-year remission and it was great.

It was scary, but I kept thinking, We can handle this. If it grows back, we'll just operate and take it out again. But in 2017 he started this deterioration where he suddenly had memory issues and started forgetting things. He had an MRI and we discovered that the tumour had not only grown back but started spreading to a part of the brain responsible for short-term memory. The doctor said, "We can't operate on this. We have to rely on drugs."

On the fifth of December, I had a call from

my aunt saying he's in critical condition in hospital, he's had a seizure, you have to come immediately. The following morning, I flew to Israel. My sister called me in transit saying the doctor asked if we can resuscitate now because we're not even sure if he is going to make it till you arrive. I was just crying in the middle of the airport in France. When I got there, he was in neurological intensive care, holding on, breathing hard, but still there. For two weeks it looked like he was managing to make a recovery. But then the doctors came and said, "Look the seizure caused fluids to get in there and they've created a lot of pressure and it is going to start hurting him soon. The only real option is we bombard him with drugs now."

So that was what happened. He was bombarded with drugs. I didn't know what the effect of this morphine would be. While I was staying with my aunt, I got a call from her saying your brother wants to talk to you. He got up. He actually sat on the bed, saying, "Hey what's up?" But it was just one day like that and after that he started suffering and they had to increase the morphine and then give him something stronger, fentanyl patches. It's a really strong drug and it suppresses the breathing mechanism, and you suffocate if you have an overdose. That's what happened to him. I was actually sitting with him and holding his hand and telling him how much I would miss him, and he just stopped breathing.

After I came back following the funeral, I

went back to swimming, because that's what makes me happy. I remember we had an ice swim in Gladhouse reservoir, completely covered in ice, in January last year. We had to break the ice and get in. I thought it helped. Every time I come out of the water, I feel better. I guess it's the endorphins. In terms of mood it does make me feel better.

Then I had another shock. Just over a month after my brother died, I got a phone call saying my aunt had killed herself. She was only six years older than me, very close to my brother and me. She'd taken it very hard. I remember she kept telling me we didn't do enough to save him. That was a big shock.

After the funeral, I was actually starting to do better, overcoming all these difficulties. I went swimming as usual, started almost a tradition of going to Gladhouse reservoir, very close to my work. I went there on a Friday after work for a dip. Sometimes someone joined me, sometimes I was all alone. I thought swimming was helping me to cope with everything.

Then my grandma passed away. She was almost ninety-one and I'd already planned to visit for her birthday. Of all the deaths we had that was the most expected, but for me it was just devastating. It felt like I was surrounded by death. I couldn't come back for her funeral. It was too short notice.

Anna, my wife, noticed something was wrong with me. I told her a week or two after my grandmother passed away, that I was thinking, something is wrong. I'm not enjoying my swimming. It's not making me happy. She got me a GP appointment and told me to go and talk with the GP. I went and told him everything that happened, and he said it sounded like I was suffering from depression.

I signed off work and started taking drugs. They are my happy pills. I took them and I went back to swimming – well, actually, I never stopped swimming; it was just the feeling afterwards wasn't there. Swimming has been very helpful this year. When the doctor gave me these pills, he said, "It's not like you take these, sit at home, watch TV and get happy. You need to do things that make you happy to get there. You need to do things, speak to people – if it makes you happy to go swimming, do that. Do things that put a smile on your face, and what these drugs will do is make the smile last longer than usual." So that's what I'm doing.

I also started seeing a psychologist. It's really interesting having someone professional telling you in words what you feel. Suddenly it bounces back from someone and it's like the whole picture. It's normal for you to feel this way and it just puts everything into place.

She referred to my dad's death as well. My dad passed away in 2011. She said that was the first one. It was still all fresh and unprocessed when my brother was diagnosed, and the only time I started processing it was when I started seeing the psychologist. My father had a heart attack without any warning and it was almost exactly a year later that my brother was diagnosed with a brain tumour. She said, 'You need to process that.'

I'm still on the antidepressants, and I'm giving it a bit more time because I don't know what will happen if I stop taking them. I'm also starting work, a phased return.

In the past few months I've done a lot of swimming. Three, four times a week, sometimes alone, sometimes with other people. It's a lifesaver. It makes me happy.

SWIMMING THROUGH TEARS

BRYONY, silversmith, Edinburgh

Not long after my mum died, I was staying with a friend in Bournemouth, and she encouraged me to go swimming with her, saying, "Your tears will mingle with the salt of the sea."

I remember thinking this was such a wonderful chance to do whatever your body needs to do, whether you need to cry loads or shout loads, or you just need to dive into the sea and be encompassed by water. It was so freeing. I've always loved diving into the water and pretending I'm a seal or a dolphin. There's something about being surrounded by it all. It's a bit muffled as well. It muffles the world.

Later that summer we went to scatter Mum's ashes on the Norfolk Broads. None of us knew beforehand that was what she wanted but she had written it down with an X marks the spot on the map. Beautiful things happened. As we scattered the ashes, suddenly these swans appeared and came past. Then, that afternoon we went to Blakeney and it was so crazily hot that we were all swimming and diving in the sea and then all these seals popped up. They were so close and getting closer and closer, and I just thought, This is too marvellous not to try and keep doing it. I have to work out how to swim back home in Scotland.

I read things into the sea and the sky, even beams of sunlight coming through clouds, or birds and feathers. I don't know if it's the vastness, or if it's the fact that no one can control the clouds, the sun or the sea. That's something I love about the sea. We're constantly trying to control things and I think it's lovely to be aware of times when you have to recognise that it's so big, so vast, there's no way you could control it.

I was thinking recently what a good death my mum's was. That term does get used a lot, but I'd never thought about it because I'd never been with anybody as they died, and never anyone as close as Mum. She'd been diagnosed with pancreatic cancer but we thought she'd got the all-clear after an operation. Then it came back with huge severity, very quickly, and she was diagnosed with four to six months. She was dead a week later. It happened very quickly, but with enough time for us all to be there. She had this incredible weekend where she had all these people round.

When she died, my stepdad, my brother and my sister and me were there, holding her hand. It's amazing to see someone's last breath. I felt like it was tangible. I felt you could actually see that last breath go up – this silvery thing. I really felt there was definitely a spirit in her body and now that was gone.

I definitely feel she's in the ether, and she's trying to communicate. She's trying to let us know that she's around and that it's okay. It's a mixture of things in nature and a synchronicity of things appearing when you're thinking about them. There are probably loads more than I notice, but I'm not always open to them because I'm sort of in my world and thinking about work and the kids.

"I started swimming after my mum passed away, and although I wouldn't say there is a direct link, I do think that if you dig deep enough everyone who is out there swimming has a story. You don't throw yourself into freezing cold water unless there's a part of you that maybe needs a little mending."

ASTER, Edinburgh

AN OCEAN LOVE-SONG

HAYLEY, student, Gloucestershire

Rich, my husband and soulmate, died at the age of thirty-seven, two days before his birthday. On the morning when we'd been due to travel to Anglesey for a week of wild swimming and walking, he had a seizure that caused his heart to stop. It took twenty-five minutes to resuscitate him, by which time he'd sustained serious brain damage.

Rich never woke from the coma and passed away three weeks later. He drew his last breath while his favourite song, "Romeo and Juliet" by Dire Straits, was playing. Despite being profoundly deaf, and unable to wear his brain stem implant hearing device while in the coma, I know Rich knew "our song" was playing.

Wild swimming has always featured in our life together. We found each other through a website for outdoorsy people and wrote for two months before meeting. Almost immediately we started talking about swimming together and discussing which wetsuits to buy. We bought those wetsuits on our first date – the same date where we started talking about marriage. We knew we'd found our missing piece.

Rich was born with NF2 – Neurofibromatosis type 2, a rare genetic condition that causes tumours, usually benign, to grow on nerve endings. He'd spent his life in and out of hospital, having surgery to remove brain and other tumours. The surgeries often resulted in paralysis of parts of his body, and the growth of tumours which were too risky to remove meant that Rich had severe neuropathy in his limbs. He was in constant pain, but I was the only one who knew that.

In cold water though, the pain dissipated. When swimming, Rich said he felt like he imagined most other people felt – free of pain, supported by the water, able-bodied. In the water, he didn't feel disabled. It didn't matter that he had no cochlears and couldn't balance very well – the water held him. It didn't even matter that he was deaf – we communicated like we always did. It was a joy to see him swim: the minute he entered the water his face and body relaxed, as the water worked its magic.

We had our last wild swimming adventure eight days before he fell ill, when we drove to the River Monnow, behind Skenfrith Castle, Monmouthshire, to greet the sunrise. It was perfect. The sun rose over the hill as we entered the water, and afterwards we cooked porridge on Rich's favourite piece of kit – a portable wood-burning stove. The wetsuits then got packed away for the following weekend sea

swimming around Anglesey. Rich enjoyed the swim so much he ordered a fleece-lined wetsuit for sea swimming in Shetland – a trip booked for September, as he didn't want to confine his swimming to the summer. That wetsuit arrived while Rich was in a coma; it now hangs in the wardrobe next to my wedding dress.

When Rich died, I knew instinctively the only thing that would stop me following him was to swim and walk. I was shaking so violently from shock, especially in the mornings, that I figured it didn't matter if I shook with cold too, so I started going down to Clevedon Marine Lake, and booked an Airbnb with its own natural swimming pool just so I could get in the water as often as I needed to. The owners were worried about me; they kept sending their dog round to check I was okay!

I still have a very special connection with Rich, as twin souls how could we not? When I'm in the water I feel like he's right there next to me, like he always was. I also feel his lived experience of being in the water – of being held and supported, and for that short time, the pain in my head and heart eases, just like the pain from the NF2 tumours eased for Rich.

I've read that water and mountains are transitional, connection-enhancing spaces, and for Rich and me those connections are definitely enhanced in water. It feels like we're together again physically, whereas out of the water I feel like I've been eviscerated, my heart cleaved in two. I also find the water helps release otherwise hidden feelings and emotions, so I'll often end up crying a few minutes after getting dressed, usually while drinking my hot Ribena.

The water has helped me find humans who want to be a part of my grief family. I don't have conventional support networks, but friends old and new have stepped up to the plate, and in many cases stepped into the water, to show how much they love and care for me and Rich.

Asking on Instagram if any fellow wild swimmers would meet up with me for a swim has resulted in friendships I think will be there for life. As a profoundly grieving person I can't be easy to spend time with, but I've been told that my sense of humour, my honesty and authenticity are still very much intact, so much so that I'm genuinely surprised when people want to meet me, and then meet up again after the first time! Wild swimming, and wild swimmers, are saving my life.

It's not yet been a year since Rich died, so it's far too early to say where wild swimming will take me, but I know it will feature strongly. I claimed the hashtag "griefswims" on Instagram, and I'm starting to meet with others who've experienced out of order bereavement, and taking them for their first wild swim, so I suspect this will become an aspect of my life's work.

When someone sends me a message saying they know how much pain I'm in, but that I'm able to take that pain with me to the water and get in, and how that in turn motivates them to go for a walk to the park when they'd previously not been able to get out of bed, then I feel like I'm doing what I should be doing. I'm helping others, even if in a very small way. Rich spent his life helping others, so I feel like it's the least I can do.

The water isn't mine to share, as it's something everyone should have access to, but I do feel a responsibility to show others what it can do, and how it can help, not heal – that's far too strong a word for those who are feeling such pain, when grief is not an illness; but the water can provide comfort. It soothes the soul.

A GAP TO SWIM THROUGH

DEREK, IT manager, Edinburgh

When my wife Karen passed away two years ago, we could hold each other's hand and she could say she wouldn't change a thing in her life. If there was something we wanted to do we did it. Never put off to tomorrow what we could do today. Looking back on her life, too short at fifty, I'm so glad we did just that. When we were told that Karen was dying her first thought was to ask me if I was okay. That's the kind of person she always was, putting others first.

After she passed away it left a huge gap in my life and I took Karen's advice to keep busy and active. I had promised her I would make the most of my life and try and help others in her memory. I'd always fancied sea swimming but I just never had the time or knew anyone else that did it, so I had to turn up one Sunday morning and introduce myself to the local swimming group. I was a bit nervous about how everyone would be, but I quickly realised they were in fact the most welcoming of groups you could ever meet. I thought it would be fun, but never realised how fulfilling it would be and quite addictive, too.

THE NEW NORMAL

GEORGE, area manager, Argyll

In October 2014 our eldest son James took his life. You go into autopilot in those first ten days following the death, and I'm afraid it was straight into funeral arrangements. I look back on it and think, "Why was I having to do all of this for my twenty-year-old son?" It does break my heart.

Life definitely changed after that. In the spring of 2015, a friend asked me to join him in a triathlon team and for me to do the outdoor swimming bit. I said okay. I thought something like that would be good for me. There was a wee swimming group over in Perthshire where I lived, about a dozen of us who called ourselves Swimming Nutters.

I've always kept fit and this was another challenge. I did the triathlon, and I was hooked by then. My friend turned around eventually and said, "George, back in January, when I asked you about the swim, I just felt you needed something." I guess I probably did.

When you're going through grief, you're not feeling that you're different from anybody else. But looking back, I see I was going through a fog. And I wonder if we're still going through the fogs. Everyone has their own challenges and this just happens to be Vic [George's partner] and my challenge. I call it the new normal – because it doesn't actually leave you. Every single day we think about James. But we have got closer and I've also got a strong Christian faith. Losing a child is a hard thing, but that has strengthened my faith.

I think about James all the time when I'm swimming. But I think about James anyway. You have time when you are on your own, swimming away and your mind just starts to think about things. It's bittersweet.

James had a mental illness and an illness killed him, in my mind. We do think he was on the high functioning end of the autistic spectrum. He didn't talk and I'm not sure if he ever would have. This is one of the bits of my story. During James's service, I used a quote from a war writer, which said that if you're willing to open up and talk about your vulnerabilities you technically open yourself to being hurt by others who might think that your feelings are really stupid. But in my experience, if you open up to others, it's amazing the stories and experiences you get back.

I work for Volkswagen and the company's charity of 2019 is Mind. I thought I would like to do something for that and the idea of doing this Four Rivers Challenge popped into my head, and that's what I'm doing to raise money. It's swimming the four rivers of the four capitals in four seasons for mental health. I do believe the inspiration came from my creator, saying go and do this.

"It's like the sea encompasses all these souls. When you go out into it, it's as if you're going out into this body of love that gives you a hug. It's a comfort. Even in cold water it hugs you more."
LESLEY, artist, East Lothian

"I have been swimming in the wilds for many years originating in my hillwalking and geology days when I'd dip in lochs and rivers. More recently it has become an activity itself, really starting when my mother was diagnosed with terminal illness and I needed something for myself that would take me away from normal life and swimming in the wild promised the rush that I wanted, in those moments when I'm in the water and the waves are at eye level I'm euphoric because it's truly beautiful."

JENNY, Edinburgh

8

THE SEA DOESN'T JUDGE

BELONGING AND BODY CONFIDENCE

THE POWER OF ACCEPTANCE

We all want to belong. Not just to fit in, but to properly be accepted for who we are, as people and bodies of whatever shape or size. Often swimmers say that when they get in that water, when they plunge down or float on their backs, they feel like this is where they belong. The sea, the loch, the river, all these wild waters seem to accept us, even if they might throw us around and spit us out again. The water makes no judgement. The seaweed, the fish, the birds, don't tell us we are too fat, thin, hairy, or not the right type of person in some way.

Anna's photographs have, along the way, prompted a lot of talk about body acceptance, confidence, even body joy. That's what many see in her images of people of wildly differing shapes and sizes, diving off a groyne at Portobello beach, doing handstands or plunging through the ice. No one seems all that very much bothered about how they look.

Of course, that's not the whole truth. Some people are indeed bothered, but just get on with it. There are also those out there who struggle with body image, at least in some parts of their lives. And there are others who really do seem genuinely at home with whatever body shape they're in.

Just as our bodies differ, so do our feelings about them. What we often hear said, though, is that people feel more comfortable about stripping down and even letting it all hang out in the wild swimming community than they would in a swimming pool. This seems particularly valuable given that, in research by the House of Commons Health Committee and the Active People's Survey, body confidence concerns and fear of judgement, have been cited as key factors in women and young girls giving up swimming and other sports. A 2019 survey by the UK social enterprise Better found that 51% of women and 36% of men were not confident in their body image.

FORGETTING THE BODY

There's an effect that can be witnessed when watching a bunch of bathers on the shore. Often they arrive, strip down, slightly coyly, stand nervously at the edge of the water, a little self-conscious. Yet, when they emerge from the full onslaught of cold and water, exhilarated, they are all smiles and laughter, unconcerned, or at least less concerned, about whether anyone may be watching – keen only to get dried down and warmed up, bits of flesh flashed here and there as they struggle from swimsuit into dry clothes.

"I'm usually just too happy and proud of myself getting in the water to think about my body," says Niamh. "There is something about the fact that everyone else is totally focused on their experience too. I've never felt watched by anyone swimming. The pride that comes from getting in overrides any nerves about bodies being on show!"

Several things may be facilitating this lack of self-consciousness around wild swimming. The act of getting in cold water is such a shock to the system that most of us have our attention directed to what's going on within our bodies and the water around us rather than what other people in our vicinity might be thinking of us. Also, once we're in the flow state (see chapter 2), the parts of our brain involved in self-awareness have reduced activity. We are not thinking so much of how we seem. We are in our moment, in the zone. Who cares if our hair is like a mop of bladderwrack or we look more like a lolloping walrus than sleek dolphin?

EMBODIED IN OUR BODIES

Some people call the state of being entirely in our bodies and engaging with the world through our senses, embodiment – and research shows a strong correlation between body appreciation and both flow state and embodiment. It seems that when we swim ourselves into that state, it feels like we belong, not only in the water, but in and to ourselves.

Swimming also makes us ask what it is these bodies of ours are built for. Wild swimmers will talk about their appreciation of the functionality of subcutaneous fat as insulation. It's good to carry a bit of blubber when you're plunging into cold water not much above zero. Edinburgh swimmer, Anne observes, "There's a reason people have body fat. There's a reason women have more of it. There is a reason women, anecdotally, do more outdoor swimming and are better at it. I say this to a lot of people, 'There's not many things this body is naturally good at,

based on their physique but this isn't at all true for swimming – especially outdoor swimming, where being bigger can improve your ability to stay in cold temperatures for longer."

Rosie set up Deakin and Blue after reading reports about the Active People Survey that found that between 2005 and 2014 half a million women in England had given up swimming. Nick Bitel, Sport England's chairman, theorised that many of these women may have stopped because they were "worried about being judged about how they looked". As Rosie points out, "You can feel very exposed or vulnerable in swimwear. For most of us it's as near to naked as we get in front of strangers."

and as it turns out being in cold water is one of them – so I'll take it.'"

Alice, a keen long-distance and ice swimmer notes, similarly, "I'm really proud of my body for what it's helped me to achieve. I can swim in really icy water and I don't get cold. Yes, it's cold. I'm not saying it isn't cold, but I'm able to cope with that. I swam the English Channel. I swam the length of Loch Lomond when it was actually pretty cold."

SWIMWEAR TO BE POSITIVE IN

There are, meanwhile, plenty of larger men and women excelling at the endurance aspects of this sport. As Rosie Cook, who founded swimwear brand, Deakin and Blue, puts it, "It's an activity where men and women of all shapes and sizes can take part at a high level. I often observe that at the beginning of a marathon you might be able to identify the fastest runner

IS SWIMMING FOR EVERYONE?

It's not just belonging in the water that swimmers talk about, it's belonging to a community that's perceived as inclusive. The people there, at the water's edge, they say, are welcoming, non-judgemental.

But are they? It's clear that, while it includes young and old, fat and thin, people with disabilities, LGBT people, the swimming community is predominantly white. This extends from swimming's grassroots to the very top. Alice Dearing, a marathon swimmer – who looks set to represent Team GB at Tokyo 2020 in the open-water swimming – is currently the team's only black swimmer. In the US, Ebony Rosemond founded Black Kids Swim to offer guidance and information for black swimmers and their families.

Alex, a swimmer who describes herself as "mixed Asian", is well immersed in the Scottish

swimming community. She says, "I'm not sure I would say the community is inclusive or exclusive. I think most people just get on with swimming – so I suppose that is a kind of inclusivity."

She has never, she says, been made to feel excluded. "But I have had one or two comments about how it's rare to see an Asian person doing open-water swimming. I think swimming is typically considered a dangerous activity in Asian countries or cultures. A child drowns every forty-five seconds in Asia as a result of unsupervised swimming so it's no surprise that this may lead to reluctance among people of this cultural background to try open-water swimming. And, for everyone, it's quite daunting to throw yourself into water where you can't see or touch the bottom or might not be able to swim to the side for a rest."

Briana is an African-American and Angolan swimmer living in Scotland. She observes that swimming of any sort can seem "incredibly white and inaccessible to BAME people". And her observation is borne out by a Swim England survey which found that fewer than 10% of 70,000 competitive swimmers identity as black. But this, Briana notes, is her own experience from within her family and community – and might not be the case for everyone.

Wild swimming is just one of many outdoor activities – including snow sports, hill-walking and camping – which, she says, are seen, in her community, as "white". Her family did sign her up for swimming lessons at a young age, but still, "They view me getting in freezing cold water to swim as something incredibly risky and most likely something that a white person would do. Taking these wild risks and engaging in life-threatening activities is not something immigrant families or black families teach their kids."

DIPPERS AND TITANS

A way in which wild swimming does feel in-clusive, is in its mixing of abilities. It is a sport in which athletic Titans mix easily with mere mortals who are just there for a gentle splash. At, for instance, the Scottish Winter Swimming Championships, dippers mix with long-distance swimmers, in races that range from a short 50 metres heads-up breaststroke (prizes for the best silly hat), to a challenging 450 metres, all taking place in water which happens to be below 4°C.

With a race category for those in their seven-ties and beyond, the Scottish Winter Swimming Championships also attracts older people – as does wild swimming in general. Eighty-year-old Sandra Lea, who only started regular open-water swimming at the age of sixty-eight, is among them. "The exercise and atmosphere of swimming with these much younger swimmers takes years off me," she says. "Even though I'm getting on a bit they all make me feel like one of them and it's great fun."

One feature that's distinct to wild swimming – as it is to other more democratically inclined sports – is that it doesn't take place in an envi-ronment built by humans for one specific type of person, whether of size, shape or abilities, rather than another. The sea is a space that feels beyond cultural constructions and expecta-tions. It offers the chance to be who or what we like there.

We can imagine, for instance, that the sea makes no judgement regarding your gender. Artist Niko describes their dream of a queer, feminist, aquatic evolution. "I dream of a trans and queer future in the water; one where we evolve back into the ocean, like whales did. We'll escape this binary-gendered, capitalist patriarchy that humans built. Contemporary culture makes living on the land really difficult for anyone that the system doesn't work for."

BUDDIES AND BANTER

The sea is, at the same time, not an environ-ment that is immediately physically accessible. Yet people with different physical disabilities are frequently found there in the water. Many swimmers report that this is thanks to the support and help of their community and their friends. Dawn, for instance, describes how when she was in so much pain she could barely walk, her friends took her down to the water and helped her in. Blind swimmer Jacky swims by either following her wife in a kayak, or with a friend who buddies alongside her.

"We all come with our different reasons," Jacky says. "None of us have to have anything in common but the water. It's all different back-grounds, all different ages, all different sizes. You've got the full range of genders, disabilities and abilities, but all that goes once you're here. And the banter and the faffing is a huge part of it. Sometimes we can be here for an hour after-wards and we're all shivering trying to drink our drinks, shaking like mad. You've got that com-monality that with some activities you don't get. We say what's said in the loch, stays in the loch. It's cathartic."

"In the sea, we're all just wildlife."
MORAG, Lochaber

"We all have beautiful bodies – in all shapes and sizes, with muscles and fat bits and stories to tell of a real life lived. Wild swimming and striding with our fellow swimmers celebrates this – men and women alike."

GILLY, ice swimmer, Lake District

BODY TALK

STRONG AND VULNERABLE

KARA, international legal advisor, Edinburgh

As someone who lives with depression and anxiety, wild swimming has had a huge, positive impact on my mental health. I feel so at peace and alive in the water. I had a miscarriage not so long ago. I felt resentment towards my new body shape and what I felt it represented at the time – failure, grief, comfort eating and a pregnant body but no baby. Wild swimming has helped me fall back in love with my body and realise just how strong, vulnerable and unique each of us are.

THE PERCEPTIONS OF OTHERS

ITAMAR, validation engineer, Edinburgh

For me it's really an issue of not caring much about how other people perceive me, especially when I'm busy trying to have fun.

A NEW ATTITUDE

MICHELLE, research data and information officer, Edinburgh

It's not so much more confidence in my body but no longer caring about being seen with very little on. I have a new-found "who gives a toss" attitude to just stripping off and getting changed in public and a realisation that nobody cares or is looking anyway.

BECOMING A WAVE

MORAG, retired nurse, Lochaber

I'm not exactly at peace with my new shape, mainly because it's unfamiliar, but also because there's far too much of me to fit in my old clothes. But none of that matters at all when I'm in the water because my body feels like it's part of the sea, the loch, the river. I just become a wave.

AT HOME IN A SELKIE SKIN

NIKO, artist, Skye

I always thought I was a mermaid. I used to roll around on the floor and only respond to the name Ariel, and I've always loved swimming in the sea – especially on family holidays to Anglesey. As a teenager I stopped enjoying swimming because I was self-conscious about my body and swimming stopped being part of my life, I guess.

At art school I met my best friend, Indigo. When we worked together in the studios, she told me stories from the Orkney islands where she grew up. I loved the selkie stories, about seal creatures that shed their skin to become human on land.

When we graduated it felt like there was this intense splitting; Indigo went back to Orkney and I went to live in Finland. At that point,

we decided to use the selkie story as a way to think about our friendship. With the North Sea between us, we imagined the water as a collaborative space, as we were no longer able to be physically close in the studio. Through the selkie stories we dreamed of reconnecting. We made our own seal skins out of felt; we imagined slipping them on and escaping from the land to be together again. This project also inspired me to start outdoor swimming again. I guess there was something about this notion of "getting back in the water". Through the stories and my outdoor swimming practice, I realised I'm actually a selkie, not a mermaid.

The selkie story has become really important to me in thinking through gender transition. Selkies have another truer form that's not seen by land folk – and I do too. It's also a really beautiful way of thinking about being at home in one's skin. When I swim outdoors, I feel free from the constraints of gender and societal expectations of my body – I am fluid and free; I feel at home in my skin. Somehow now I've ended up on Skye, where I have this strange summer job selling tickets for seal-watching tours; it's the perfect temp-job for a selkie!

Selkie stories have provided me with a way to hold on to my truth, even when it's denied by the world. In many of these tales, the selkie has their skin stolen by somebody on the land because they want to keep them or fix them in their human form. I want to be allowed to be in this fluid space, in this between space; in a fluid embodiment that isn't fixed. It's not about being one thing or another, or about being in this place, or that one. It's about being both, and always in motion between those things. Making my own seal skin is a kind of activist action that rejects this violent "fixing" of the land; I felt my means of escape to the fluid spaces of the sea.

A CHAMPION AT EIGHTY

SANDRA, retired, Inverness

I'm still quite a strong swimmer but a lot slower these days. I guess that's to be expected when you're in your eightieth year. But I do feel more mentally alert, fitter, healthier and happier because of my wild swimming. I swim in open water two or three times a week. Whenever someone in the Wild Highlanders posts that they're swimming somewhere, I go too!

My mum taught me to swim in the sea at Inverness when I was very young. I had a home-made, hand-knitted swimsuit. You can imagine what happened when it got wet! It wasn't considered open-water or wild swimming, though – it was just "going to the beach". We did our "proper" swimming in the pool not in the sea. I didn't start wild swimming till twelve years ago.

I did swim in the sea now and again in my early years, but folk thought I was mad because it was freezing so I didn't advertise my wee trips to the sea. In my early years in the 1940s and 1950s it was all pool swimming for us with one exception. That was the Annual Kessock Ferry swim in Inverness. It was the highlight of the year and the whole town turned out to watch. To us it wasn't wild swimming, it was simply a challenge. My first Kessock ferry crossing was in 1948 at the age of eight.

I love the freedom and diversity of the open water whether it's in the sea or one of our many beautiful lochs. I feel at one with nature out in the open. Mother Nature has many faces whether you're in the sea or the loch. I swim back crawl a lot so I don't miss much. The scenery up here in the Highlands is amazing.

I think wild swimming is a great sport, mentally and physically, especially for older people. The muscles are supported in the water and it's one of the safest exercises. I have bad arthritis and always feel a lot better after a swim in the cold water. It seems to relieve all my stress and strain. I believe it also boosts the immune system. We come out on a high and, with hot chocolate, cake and good company, I feel on top of the world.

BEING BACK IN YOUR BODY

ANNE, GIS analyst, Edinburgh

Some people say swimming is the only time they don't feel self-conscious. But that's not the case for me. I'd done a lot of work in dealing

with body image before I started swimming. But it's wonderful to go along to swim and feel everyone else not caring either.

There are situations where I do feel self-conscious but it's not swimming, and if it is, it's definitely not outdoors. I remember hearing the swimmer Ella Foote saying in an interview that if she has to get all dolled up for a night on the town, she would feel self-conscious, whereas if she was to get on a train in a swimming costume, she wouldn't care. I don't know if I would get on a train in my swimming costume, but I would definitely strip off on Portobello beach and not care. It took work to get to this point, but I now work on the principle that the only time it's worth feeling self-conscious about something is when there's a need to look good doing it. Swimming is so practical. I'm not here as a visual thing for anyone else.

When we're getting changed, I look up the groyne and I don't necessarily see a huge range of physiques, I just see a load of people. The minute differences we obsess over just don't show in a crowd.

It took me a long time to get to the point where I self-describe as fat and see it as a neutral descriptor, not a bad thing. The big turning point for me was that I had a back injury and so I had to do some exercise to recover from that. What I needed to do to help me recover forced me back into my body, in the way that swimmers talk of being forced back into their bodies. Being forced to be present.

Ten years ago, this would have been a very different conversation and I probably would not have started swimming. I have got myself to the point I don't have to feel like my body is the window on my soul. I can just use it for what it needs to be used for. My body does what I need it to do – and when it doesn't, it's because I'm unfit, not because I'm fat. My body is the vehicle that gets me to the place in the sea where I get to feel that hit. When you have pursuits that are so deeply physical, you have to appreciate your body. Without this cumbersome meat-prison, we wouldn't be able to get in the sea!

When you're in a body you don't like, it's easy to have all these hobbies that are quite cerebral – you read, you watch TV. You do things that don't require movement, and so that just takes you further and further away from your relationship with your body. Having that back injury shocked me into my body. I had to deal with having a body, which meant I had to deal with appreciating it. Once you've got one pursuit that is a physical thing, like swimming, you can do other things, and you realise, "Oh wait, all of these outdoor hobbies and sports, they're not just for fit people – they're for anyone who wants to get out and do them and can find exercise gear in their size."

It was a revelation that my body can do things – and it's something you can't force anyone into. You can't make anyone like exercise. You need that catalyst that makes you realise there's a lot of things your body can do – and I really like the idea that for a lot of people that might be swimming. Because, what a thing to use your body for!

SWIMMING AS COUNTERBALANCE

ZOE, stage manager, Edinburgh

After three years of trying to conceive, discovering I have fertility problems, a surprise pregnancy and a devastating miscarriage I was advised to find something to look forward to. A challenge that I can complete, that will fulfil and distract me. Swimming really fitted the bill and I decided to challenge myself to swim in fifty-two different places in a year. I'm seeing the most beautiful places on my journey. It makes me feel calm, happy and at one with the world. It makes me feel like I fit in. I'm about to have IVF by myself, to become a solo mum by choice. Trying to conceive by myself can feel quite isolating and this is the counterbalance.

SWIMSUIT SUPERPOWER

ELLA FOOTE, swimmer and journalist

Women often message me, or comment, "I could never do what you do, you're so brave." If they were referring to me plunging into cold water, wading through mud, letting weeds tangle around my legs or getting up close and personal to the pond life . . . I could sort of understand, even accept the bravery badge. However, more often than not, they go on to say, "Putting on a swimsuit, let alone having your photo taken. I couldn't do it!"

I would be lying if I said I loved my body and didn't care what I looked like in my swimsuit. I haven't mastered the art of acceptance and peace when it comes to my figure. But once I have wriggled into my swimsuit and ensured the nipples are facing up and out (thanks for that tip, Mum), I don't care any more. I look what I look like and the water doesn't care. In fact, better than that, the water embraces me like nothing else. As I slip into a river, lake, pond or ocean I am carried. The water swirls around

my fleshy figure, hugs it and supports me on my journey. A little dip or a lengthy trip, it pushes me forward – I stroke it in return. Brackish, salty, silky, silty or dreamlike clarity – the water loves my body.

On land I feel clumsy and my movement is laboured, in the water I feel like a wisp. I have perfected my starfish, breasts and belly pointing to the sky. I can scoop the water away while I chatter to pals doing breaststroke. I have strength in my arms and shoulders to deliver a strong and consistent front crawl, barely getting out of breath, swimming accidental distances down a river or along the coast. A playing field isn't a leveller; only in water do I feel I can achieve what my slender peers can, sometimes even better them. But that isn't what it is about.

I can't tell you to love your body, but why not start with liking it. It is yours. Tattoo it, tan it, pierce holes or slather it in lotion, just look after it. Notice the strength of it, how it breathes for you without you even asking it to. Watch how it guides you through life at all shapes, sizes and forms it takes on as you grow. I can tell you this, everyone else is so consumed with their own body, they won't notice yours and if they do, it is to see the things they wish they had, the things they love about your funny body.

The only way to love yourself in your swimsuit, is to love the suit itself. Don't settle for something short in the body, or tight in the bust. If it disappears into your bottom or chafes your armpits, it isn't going to make you feel good. Don't settle for a cheap piece of fabric that does the job. Seek out the suit that makes you feel sexy. Explore the colours, patterns and variety on offer, try them all on! Swimsuits are like a second skin, so choose wisely, allow it to help you love the skin you're in.

People have called this image of seventy women walking into the sea for International Women's Day "the barcode of happiness". In March 2019, we teamed up with body positivity activist Danni Gordon to organise a dip celebrating solidarity, body confidence and diversity. We were amazed at the numbers who turned out at our local beach, Wardie Bay. Temperatures on that morning were below 6°C.

GETTING THAT BODY CONFIDENCE

DANNI GORDON, body positivity activist, the Chachi Power Project

Recent research shows that body confidence issues affect the majority of the population to some degree. And it's not just a women's issue – all genders are suffering. Here are my top five tips for your body confidence journey. Hopefully they will make an impact in your relationship to your body. And remember: everybody's body is a bikini (or a trunks) body!

1. Practice some much needed self-compassion. Start being kinder to yourself in the mirror. Use gentler, more neutral words like "soft" or "round" or "rippled" rather than "gross" or "ugly". Use affirmations if that is your bag. Shouting "You are Beautiful! You are hot! You are gorgeous!" in the mirror every day may seem ridiculous but your brain can re-mould and this is a great way to help it do that.

2. Start learning about the Body Positive Movement. Follow more diverse body shapes online. Unfollow the accounts that breed shame and comparison. Get right in among the Movement and educate yourself. There are some excellent and diverse wild swimmers out there. Follow them online!

3. Don't buy the unhelpful magazines, don't hang out with the toxic aunties, don't let people talk about your body. Your energy and your body is sacred. Start treating it with respect and demand that others treat it that way too.

4. If weight is the body "issue" you have fought with then don't be sucked into the diets that promise you happiness. Peace is better than happiness and diets are just another battle designed to make you think you are weak or a failure so you keep coming back for more. Stop bringing more battles into your life. Perhaps look into the concept of "Intuitive Eating" to get a different handle on your relationship to food and your body.

5. And here is the golden nugget . . . if you do nothing else, heed these words. Stop saying negative things out loud about your own and anyone else's body. Stop putting that energy out there. Stop taking part in those "bonding" conversations about how your cellulite is worse than your friends'. Stop gaining a second of pleasure by bad-mouthing someone's clothes or hair or body type. It's just adding to the toxicity we already experience every day. This is the one act which is your sure-fire way to successfully rewire your brain. The truth is: if you think everyone is criticising you it's probably because you are criticising everyone else.

SWIMMING THROUGH THE AGES

LARA MILWARD, award-winning fitness coach and author of the *Sunday Times* Fit as A Fiddle

Age is often seen as decline. Age is often seen as frailty. Neither of these need apply if we change the language we use about ourselves and if we change our lifestyle.

As we age, we see many changes in our body composition and our hormones. Some people will see more change than others for we are all unique, but all studies and research point to the fact that exercise is vital to physical and mental wellbeing in our later years. Naturally we lose some muscle mass (sarcopenia) and bone density (osteopenia), but resistance exercise, both bodyweight and weighted, can help disrupt this scenario.

Water is over 700 times denser than air and provides great resistance for your muscles without the impact of running, say, as you remove gravity. Swimming is effectively pulling your body through a dense liquid using all your body's muscles as well are your cardiovascular system. It is actually the perfect exercise.

Age is no barrier and no excuse. If you want to try wild swimming or any new sport, just do it. Don't think too hard about it; face the fear and do it anyway. You won't regret it.

9

COLD
COMFORT

SWIMMING AWAY
THE PAIN

"What struck me is that I didn't feel pain. That was the first time in years that I hadn't felt any pain. As soon as the cold water hit, I stopped feeling pain."

KARIN, Cairngorms

AN ICE-BREAKER

Dawn pats the surface of the reservoir, gently breaking the area ahead of her so she can walk in. Glass this fine has sharp edges and though it's possible to wade straight through it, the result is cuts and scratches, often barely felt as the water is numbingly cold.

The ice is her plaything. She revels in it, running her hands underneath its millimetre-thick surface, and attempting to lift up fragments. Glass-like shards split and crack as she tries to lift them up into the air. They slip away from her. But she masters the technique and soon she is holding up large panes, peering through them, laughing, dropping them from up high above her head, so that they fall and shatter down over her arms.

A decade ago, Dawn wouldn't have been able to do any of this. She would barely have been able to walk down to the water and required a stick or wheelchair to get about. For ten years she suffered so terribly from pain – following a back injury, but also associated with the genetic condition Ehlers-Danlos syndrome – that she would be unable to leave her house, or bed. She was, in her late thirties, "medically retired" from work.

At one point she was so depressed she came close to suicide. "The majority of the problem was pain," she recalls. "I got to the stage where I couldn't go on any longer. It wasn't a planned suicide; it was just that the pain was so bad I'd taken all my tablets. I have a daughter. I'm so pleased it didn't work."

The pain isn't entirely gone now. There are still flare-ups. But she deals with them. One of the key ways she does this is through cold-water swimming. "That's my medication now," she says. She has long been on strong opiate medication, but she is working her way towards coming off it, and has already halved her dose.

Dawn came to wild swimming in 2016. She was just getting back on her feet and had returned to a job at a charity, when one day a colleague asked what her next goal was going to be. She joked "to swim the Channel". Within weeks she had been introduced to swim coach, Debbie Kelso, and was trying her first swim. She recalls that she had "never smiled so much in her entire life" as she did on that swim. "I came out and I buzzed till my next swim."

Soon she had become close friends with Debbie, and was also heading off on swim safaris across Scotland with a local group of swimmers. On one of these, she recalls, she had a revelation about how much the water really was helping. At first crippled by pain, she found, over a series of dips, that it was disappearing. The more she swam, the more it went away. "I've no idea why it happens," Dawn says. "I do wonder if it's because I'm so numb that I'm managing to move more which then stops me going into spasm. I think because it's so cold, it reduces inflammation and then allows me to move and then stops the pain getting worse."

GETTING INTO COLD WATER

The problem with writing about pain and cold-water swimming is that the research into the physiological mechanisms is still in its infancy. Athletes such as marathon runners have long extolled the virtues of the ice bath in enabling them to deal with punishing training schedules, but in research terms all we have are occasional

case studies rather than big controlled scientific trials.

Yet, in medical and scientific circles there is a growing interest in whether regular cold-water immersion may help reduce the pain and inflammation associated with certain chronic conditions. One case study, for instance, published in the *British Medical Journal* in 2018, looked into the experience of a man who decided to see if cold-water swimming would help relieve the constant pain he'd suffered since having facial surgery.

The pain, he reported, disappeared after swimming. "Once I was in the water," he said, "I had tunnel vision. For the first time in months, I completely forgot about the pain or the fear of shooting pains in my chest if I moved."

TAKING OUR PAIN TO THE WATER

It's this kind of chronic pain that is at the heart of the *Taking the Plunge* project. From the moment we started, the personal stories of such cold-water relief gripped us. Even if pain wasn't the reason why people were choosing to swim, they were certainly reporting benefits – people like Lil, who found relief from the ache of her fibromyalgia, and said that following a swim she will "just dance".

Pain also was one of the reasons Anna was there. "My joints," she would say, "are at times stiff to the point of being unable to operate a camera, pen, computer or car, my fatigue levels are high. My pain levels can be excruciating. My body is literally fighting itself." But, the cold

which itself is at the root of a lot of health problems."

Among the mechanisms via which cold water may be working to reduce inflammation, is what's called the "diving reflex". That's what happens, Mark says, when you put your face in cold water and trigger a huge stimulation of both parts of your autonomic nervous system which controls your unconscious body processes – the parasympathetic and sympathetic branches. It's set off by chilling and wetting the nostrils and face while breath-holding. Messages are sent out through the parasympathetic nervous system that put your organs into "rest and digest" mode, lowering heart rate and reducing inflammation. But also, at the same time the chemicals, serotonin and noradrenaline are released, and it's believed that these turn on the pain-inhibiting pathways in the brain.

Of course, inflammation isn't in and of itself a bad thing. It's an essential element in the immune system's response to infection by foreign organisms like bacteria or virus, and mostly our friend – there when we need to heal wounds or fight disease. It's only when it takes place in the absence of disease or injury, at a chronic low level, over time, that it becomes our foe.

In some diseases like rheumatoid arthritis, inflammatory bowel disease and fibromyalgia, even heart disease, inflammation runs amok – and in the absence of foreign invaders, the body can end up fighting itself. And, increasingly, it is being found to be at the heart of our chronic health problems. Inflammation, not wear and tear, is even being seen as a key aspect of ageing – so much so that some scientists have come up with the term inflammaging for the low-grade inflammation associated with age.

water was offering her relief. "I have sometimes hobbled down to the beach for my Sunday swim in terrible pain, but walked uphill all the way home feeling wonderful."

What was happening, we wondered, when people took their pain to the water?

THE DIVING REFLEX

One person who may have some possible answers is Mark Harper, a consultant anaesthetist and cold-water swimmer who is part of a team at the University of Portsmouth, driving research into the benefits of cold-water immersion.

"Cold-water swimming appears," he says, "to be one way of dealing with inflammation,

"Swimming clears my body and mind and leaves me buzzing. I'm very familiar with the physiological benefits of cold-water immersion from a sports perspective, having played Touch Rugby for Scotland during the past decade. Post-match ice baths were a critical part of our daily schedule at multi-day tournaments to aid recovery, wherever we are in the world and regardless of the air temperature!"

ALI, finance lawyer, Edinburgh

THE SCIENCES OF SWIMMING

A recent survey Mark and his colleagues conducted through the Outdoor Swimming Society supports his theory that cold water is helping people by reducing inflammation. They put out a request for a response from people who considered themselves to be self-medicating with cold-water swimming.

Mark anticipated around thirty or forty responses. He also anticipated that they would come from people with long-term conditions involving inflammation. What he got was around six hundred replies, two-thirds of which were swimming for mental health – the rest, were for physical conditions. He was stunned.

He recalls, "It was all the things we predicted. Stuff related to inflammation. Inflammatory bowel disease, fibromyalgia, PTSD, all these things. The list of things people came back saying they self-medicated for was identical to what we expected."

Cold-water therapy, of course, isn't a new idea – but it's perhaps something that's been lost, or has fallen out of fashion. Back in the 18th century, sea swimming, especially during winter, was recommended for the treatment of a range of diseases. Whole seaside resorts were founded on these perceived health benefits.

We still, centuries later, await firm scientific evidence, but anecdotes abound of cold water's pain-relieving benefits. Dawn, for instance, whose turnaround has been phenomenal – from struggling to walk to hiking up to the shelter hut halfway up Ben Nevis and summiting the iconic Suilven. The day after her Ben Nevis climb, she cancelled her disability benefit. "I thought, you're no longer disabled. I've done that walk

and I've done the Cobbler. Huge, huge achievements for me. But, if it wasn't for the swimming community, they wouldn't have happened."

Similarly, Dawn hopes to come off her medication. "I actually don't think I need it. I know I'm not in pain, so why am I taking opiate painkillers? I'm addicted unfortunately. I've been on this medication for ten years and for that time I constantly said I was in the worst pain ever."

She still has flare-ups, but now when she gets sore, she goes for a swim, helped down to the shoreline, if she is struggling, by friends. Two things have turned her life around – open-water swimming and the Thistle Foundation, an organisation helping people living with lifelong conditions for which she now works. What Dawn is currently trying to do is pass on her hope to other people. "We can't change your condition, but what we can change is how we live with your condition. If someone had said that to me ten years ago, I might not have been medically retired."

A QUIET SEA ENERGY

LIL, artist, East Lothian

I suffer from fibromyalgia which has brought me a lot of fatigue and negative feelings about my body's capabilities. I couldn't sustain a full-time job because I have to keep a keen eye on how much energy I've got. But I've got that down to a fine art now. If I know I've got a busy day ahead then I have to be careful. There's something about getting in the sea that instantly recharges and refills. I might be tired afterwards, but it's a different kind of tired. It gets rid of the pain. I get in the water feeling sore and fatigued and come out with a quiet new energy.

AS LONG AS YOU KEEP SWIMMING

KARIN, housewife, Cairngorms

The first cold-water swim I did was about three hundred yards in a lochan. It was 14°C and I thought it was Baltic – I now know different. What struck me was that I didn't feel pain. That was the first time in years I hadn't felt any pain. As soon as the cold water hit, I stopped feeling pain.

Before that I had been having a really tough time with my chronic fatigue and fibromyalgia and I was managing to do maybe ten or twelve minutes of a walk – that was about my limit – before having to rest for maybe two hours before I could do anything else. But I met someone when we were both out walking the dog and she told me about this TV programme about the wild swimming and how the cold water seemed to be beneficial.

I spoke to my friend, who was a GP, about it, but I was very daunted. I was about three stone heavier than I am now and I couldn't for the life of me imagine myself in a wetsuit with all these people I didn't know. So, my friend Michelle went and bought herself a wetsuit and arranged that first swim. That was a Wednesday night, and then on the following Sunday I loved it so much, I took myself down to Loch Morlich to swim with the regular group there.

Up to that point with things like brushing my teeth I'd have to stop midway through because I get that sort of lactic burn in my shoulders. I couldn't hang the washing on a line because I couldn't peg up more than one item at a time. But in the cold water I don't get pain. I just don't get it. Then, when I get out, depending how cold the water has been and how long I've been in, I can have a few hours of just not hurting.

I've been swimming now for about two and a half years and I've probably had fibromyalgia about fifteen years in total, and alongside it depression. Before I had fibromyalgia and chronic fatigue, my coping mechanism for stress or anything that was going on in my life was exercise. I would do body combat, anything to get me out of my own head. Then when I developed chronic fatigue, I couldn't get out. I didn't have the energy to exercise and I had no way of getting out of my own head. You're stuck in the house and all you've got to think about is yourself. I had periods in hospital because I was so low. I was in a dark place.

But when I started doing the cold-water swimming, I came off the opiates, I came off my antidepressants. That was the first time in twenty-five years I hadn't been on an antidepressant. I'd been through everything they could possibly think of – modern ones, old ones – and nothing helped. Then when I started swimming, because I could get out of my own head – even if it's just for five minutes, ten minutes, when all you're thinking about is, *God, am I going to survive this cold?* – it had such benefits. My consultant psychiatrist, whose supervision I'd been under for eight years signed me off. He said, you don't need to come any more, as long as you keep swimming.

It's now part of my official health plan. When I see my GP, it's the first thing she asks. How many times a week are you swimming? If I'm unwell, as far as being depressed goes, she tells me to get in at least once a week. Try and get in twice.

I've gone from not being able to walk more than twelve minutes, to my biggest swim last year being 3.4km. I can swim for that distance and, okay, I'm tired and getting sore by the end of it, but it's nothing compared with trying to brush my teeth when I'm warm.

My husband is constantly asking, are you not going swimming today? When were you last swimming? He knows I need the swimming. We're going to move house, but he didn't want to move anywhere that would take me too far away from this swimming community. Everything now seems to revolve around me being able to swim – it's what's keeping me well.

I would never have spoken about my mental health issues before – would never have done

it. But now I feel that if it's helped me, if swimming can help just one other person from even thinking suicidal thoughts or anything like that, then yeah, I'll tell my story to anyone.

RUNNING DOWN TO THE LOCH

MARGARET, photographer, Loch Ness

Eight years ago, I split up with my husband and that was an intensely stressful period of my life. I ended up with chronic migraines which just took over. The first one I had was the day we were splitting up – and then it just continued and got worse and worse. I was trying to work as a wedding photographer and keep things together. But I would have a headache for a few days and the next migraine would come and it would be one after the other. I had to keep working; I didn't have a choice.

I was trying to find a non-pharmaceutical cure and one of the things I noticed helped was when I went wild swimming with a journalist friend in Scotland. We went in the sea in April and it stopped the pain I got in the shoulders, which refers to the head, which creates the migraine. After that I started running down to the loch on a day when I wanted to get rid of the pain. I'd just jump in the loch and I'd feel a bit better after. It wasn't out of a desire to start wild swimming, although I really love swimming and I really love surfing and paddleboarding.

I think it's the cold – and I think it's when it's directly on the skin. It doesn't work as well when you've got a wetsuit on. If I use a wetsuit it doesn't seem to have as much impact.

That was where it started and now I do it

because I love it. I still have to live a restricted healthy lifestyle. I have to watch what I eat and do enough exercise and make sure I go out-doors. That keeps me healthy now. So, it's not always to kill the pain. I'm so much better now it doesn't bother me so much.

I have tried Ayurvedic medicine and I think that's the one thing that has brought health back to me. You've got to find your own way. Whatever keeps your stress levels down is really important; stress is definitely what triggered my health problems. I think stress is the thing that triggers many people's health problems.

For me, one of the really significant things has been being outside, walking in nature – and being completely immersed in it. Swimming takes it one step further. It's like you're releasing all the tension into the water. I tend to swim alone. I thrive on time alone. I'm a really strong swimmer but I do have a swim buoy that I tie to me. I'm asthmatic and I put my inhaler and my

phone in it. I don't swim too far. It's not about swimming distances.

That first swim was in the middle of the night. We got in and it was just Baltic. The swimming isn't what I remember about it, but the standing by the fire afterwards, thinking this is a nice feeling. You do it for that feeling, you don't always do it for the feeling when you're in there.

A GOOD SLEEP AFTER A GOOD SWIM

NEIL, IT engineer, Cairngorms

I've had a long-standing back problem – since I was fourteen. It was caused by a dehydrated disc. The sac of fluid surrounding the disc got punctured and it's likely to have happened playing rugby. But it took quite a while for it to be diagnosed and I wasn't operated on until I

was twenty. After that I had quite a few years' relief from the pain. But since 2007 it has gone downhill, to the point where I was taking daily painkillers.

But the past few months, I'm sleeping better and part of that is because I've managed to drop a lot of weight, and because of the swimming. The last two years I've had what's called root denervation where they put an electrode in to let your spine pass on an electric current into the nerve root and it gives about six or seven months of relative pain-free time. This year was good and I've been trying to up the exercise quite a lot, get to the gym and swim.

I do notice cold-water swimming helps my back quite a bit. As the denervation wore off, I started taking painkillers again. But I'm not taking a huge amount this year, because I'm overall feeling better. I've lost a chunk of weight, I'm feeling good about myself and that mental stimulation of being out on the water helps.

I also sleep better. I've had issues waking up in the night for years – my sleep pattern has been totally shot. But I know I will sleep better on a night after I've been in the water. I know that every Sunday night, after my Sunday swim, I'm going to have a good sleep. It means that going into the Monday you're starting the week with a better rest.

A SWIMMING FULL STOP

SARAH, swimming coach and Pilates teacher, Cairngorms

I was diagnosed with costochondritis in June 2018. My dad sadly passed away ten years beforehand – and for the anniversary year I thought, I'm going to challenge myself. I'm going to do an ultra-marathon, and my first half Ironman – Starman Night Triathlon. And a

five or ten km swim. But during the course of training, I realised I was really struggling with running, and I had to pull out of the ultra and the triathlon. It was then that I learned that I had costochondritis, which is inflammation of the connecting tissues in the sternum. The pain I feel can radiate down to the lower ribs, into my back and all the way up the chest. On and off, I must have been dealing with it for a long time. It can be caused by either a virus or a direct injury and I've had both. One day it can be really acutely painful and the next it can be okay, a bit like a rollercoaster.

I went from being so active, running, cycling, skiing, winter mountaineering, to having to curtail all that. I found the only thing I could do without pain is swimming; I completed my first 10km swim in September 2018.

I totally advocate if you are in pain and you feel comfortable getting in the water to go with someone else and give it a try. It might work, it might not. I don't think it necessarily cures it, but it definitely helps. It puts a full stop in somewhere. It gives you a break from whatever is going on in your busy brain.

STAYING ALIVE IN THE WATER

NIKO, artist, Skye

I've had a number of quite serious illnesses. I had malaria as a teenager and then meningitis, which was very scary. I nearly died. Later, I had glandular fever; that was the most difficult because it's such a long-term sickness. With that, it was really difficult to do anything at all. Now, I think I probably have lower energy levels than other people but I'm lucky to have made a pretty good recovery, and all this sickness has caused me to be very anxious about my health. If I have any pain at all, I jump to the conclusion that I am dying, or very seriously ill, because this has been a reality in the past. When I'm in the water none of this fear is present, because my body is experiencing so many other sensations. I guess I have to be so focused on swimming, keeping afloat, there's a different urgency to "staying alive" in the water, there's no time to be worried about a slightly achy shoulder or a bit of a tickly throat.

I'm a very body-focused person and definitely a hypochondriac. When I'm in the water I have freedom from body-based anxieties. I think many people who wild swim share my experience of using it to move through, or cope with, sickness or disability. Wild swimming can provide an escape from the tensions and

pains your body holds and will also make you feel strong. When I am in the water, I feel like I am seaweed. I love seaweed! I have been thinking a lot about how seaweed is brittle and fragile when it is dried out on the shoreline, but becomes fluid and strong in the water; that's how I feel about being a wild swimmer.

FEELING STRONG

KATIE, charity fundraiser, Edinburgh

I've always swum. Swimming pools have been part of my life for as long as I can remember. I swam for Scotland at junior and senior level, throughout school and university. Then, in my early twenties severe back problems meant I faced an operation, or stop swimming, and so I fell away from swimming – every so often I'd go back into the pool but it was a love/hate

relationship. The smell of chlorine, while so familiar, was something I hated. It was too easy to just "not go" after years of dedication.

A rollercoaster of health problems hit me in my adult life, including polycystic ovary syndrome, a molar pregnancy (very rare cancerous tumour) and a late missed miscarriage. A genetic condition called haemochromatosis, in which there is too much iron in the blood, meant weekly bloodletting in hospital. I suffered from acute urticaria and viral meningitis. Basically, my health was in freefall; and endless hospital stays and endless bouts of illness forced me to re-evaluate my lifestyle.

My second pregnancy was difficult; I was diagnosed with birth trauma from the birth of my daughter. I lacked strength from years of health problems. I tried maintaining fitness but even getting to the pool took energy that I just didn't have. I was used to being strong and physically fit. Looking back, it was most likely a form of burnout and exhaustion – both physical and mental.

After my son was born, I had post-natal anxiety and severe memory problems; it was beyond "baby brain". I was chronically tired and knew something wasn't right. I was lucky – I made some wonderfully brilliant local friends and one of them, Anna, got me into the open water. I'd done it before, but it had never crossed my mind that this could be the gentle, healing activity I needed. Then last year I was diagnosed with functional neurological disorder – a cognitive impairment problem, as a result of trauma to the head, the meningitis I suffered, and past traumatic experiences. Everything fell into place. Recovery is slow – I need to rest, rebuild and focus. But I will get there. Slowly.

Wild swimming makes me feel strong again. And I've felt healthier than I have in years. It gives me time. It switches my mind off and there's only me, and the water. Sometimes friends. And the occasional jellyfish. It reminds me that my body can do this and is something to be celebrated, instead of something that has let me down in the past. And it lets me show my daughter strength, fearlessness, and delight. At six years old she now follows me in.

THE COLOURS OF THE SEA

KATHIE, journalist, Oban

I first started wild swimming in Yorkshire, when I'd be out on walks. Usually, then, it was with most of my clothes on. I would just go in. I would be out on a walk and sometimes I couldn't resist the pull of the water. I would need to go in. I would be taken by the look of the place, Janet's Foss, for instance, with its waterfall, and maybe the idea that fairies lived there as well. Then I came to live here on the west coast of Scotland, where the coast is just amazing, and I always thought part of coming to live here would be to make the most of what you've got.

I dislocated my knee a few years ago, and my confidence in mobility was knocked. It was a limiting injury. There were certain places, certain terrains I wouldn't want to go, because I was scared I would fall.

But when I'm in the water I do feel safe. I feel there is so much freedom there. There's no pain in the water at all. When I'm in the water and I'm moving around I feel like a little mermaid. I can sort of spin round and do more. I think of the sea, being in the water, as a great healer – and it's almost like a cleansing ritual for me. It's not just the physical side. It's the mental side too. Anything you're thinking about on land, as soon as you're in the water, you've left the land and lumber behind. For me it's that immersion, the thrill of getting into the water is just unbeatable. I like getting in and moving through the water and seeing the colours.

10

SPLISH
SPLASH
SPLOSH

THE WILD ART OF
HAVING FUN

"This is grown-ups getting the chance to play with no rules, and this is so important in this target driven age in which we live."

RICHARD, Edinburgh

JOYFULNESS

Laughter ripples out on the water. The sea, says one swimmer, tickles. It makes us squeal, smile, grimace, shriek whoop and scream. When we're there it can seem like we become children again, simply playing. Splashing, as if we were toddlers, plunging into puddles.

What's striking about many of the wild swimming groups is that so many of their gatherings revolve around some kind of daft mucking about – mass handstands, skinny dips, Easter bonnet swims, the so-called Fife salute (a baring of breasts while facing the paps of Fife), silly hats, spontaneous post-swim conga dances.

You would think, at times, these adults, some of them in their sixties, seventies and even older, with their ankles stuck up in the air, were a bunch of kids. But often it turns out that they're serious adults with difficult jobs – people involved in children's mental health, international conflict resolution. All throwing themselves into the fun. A significant percentage of wild swimmers appear to be there for the play above all else.

Laughter, it's long been said, is the best medicine – and there is now evidence that un- controllable laughter is good for us, releasing endorphins which not only generate mild eu- phoria, but also dull pain.

But play, itself, is also hugely important not just in children, but as an adult activity. Dr Stuart Brown, founder of the National Institute of Play in the United States, described, in a 2008 TED talk how, "Nothing lights up the brain like play. Three-dimensional play fires up the cerebel- lum, puts a lot of input into the front lobe, the executive portion, helps contextual memory be developed . . ."

Brown believes that play is something we have lost too much from our adult culture. "The thing," he says, "that is so unique about our species is that we're really designed to play throughout our whole lifetime." We are what he calls neotenous creatures. This means that we maintain immature characteristics throughout our whole lives – play being one of them. Play, he says, is at the heart of our adaptability.

The opposite of play, he also observes, is not work, it's depression. One of the things Brown advises people do, if they want to find passion in their adult lives, is look back into their his- tories and find their own early memories of pleasure in play.

A WILD AND WATERY PLACE FOR PLAY

The water, of course, is one place where we play. For many of us, our play memories are in wild water. Talk to any swimmer about what they love about what they do and often they will mention idyllic or joyful times from childhood spent on the beach or pottering in a stream. That time they smashed the ice on a loch, splashed through a ginormous puddle, or tried to jump over a pool. "So much of the pleasure," says Bryony, a silversmith, "is about playing and just being a kid."

"Wild swimming," Helen, a management consultant, observes, "reconnects us to play in a way that other physical activities and sports don't. Having sand or gravel between your toes, not being confined to lanes or restricted by pool rules and just being in the water for pleasure, brings out the kid in us. And what kid doesn't like a bit of dress-up? Also, with wild swimming

"At the Wild Ones, we have always been about the fun – about doing handstands and silly synchronised swimming routines. The fact that we've kept that is really important to me, that it doesn't get too serious. My dad swam and he has an amazing sense of fun. He is now really ill and he can't swim, so I always think about him when we're doing all the fun stuff.

I'm really against the commodification and commercialisation of swimming and that partly comes from the big organised events – this idea that you must have a wetsuit and other equipment, you must do this and you must do that. It's always been really important to me that we are open to all kinds of swimmers, the ones that want to pootle around and the ones that get their heads down – that we don't turn into a serious swimming group."

SARAH, company director, Edinburgh

there's no performance anxiety, so you can relax and be more playful. Handstands and larking about feel like par for the course. Perhaps we're all a little bit exhibitionist too!"

Why do we swim? Do we do it because we think it's good for us? Sometimes, perhaps – when we know, for instance, it provides relief from pain. But for most people that's not the motivation. Children don't think about how good it is for them before they jump into the waves. They just dive in. They do it out of curiosity, because of some inner drive, and because it makes them feel joy.

It's the same with most wild swimmers. They do it because they can think of nothing else that gives them quite the same brilliant thrill – or makes them feel quite so giddily alive. They do it because it's fun.

A RADICAL ACT OF DEFIANCE

CHRIS, web developer, Portobello

With our particular group, we share a lot in terms of values – and that's not by design. That's just what happened. Within our group, which is part of the Wild Ones, it seems as if there's a dimension of caring about connection and caring about the natural world, and a really strong sense of playfulness. We do all these mad things like pretend synchro swims. Handstands are really important. We've built up a kind of shared culture.

For me it almost becomes an act of defiance. We're in this situation at the moment where we're faced with so many dreadful things going on – the impending destruction of the world as we know it. And, for me it's a really radical act in the face of that to continue doing something fun and joyful and connecting with nature while we still can – and connecting to people. So that's a political focus, to continue to do this despite the things that could just lead you to despair.

our swim trip. The next day she brought along her friend to the swim, and he played his drum. It was February in the Peak District and this deep fog descended on the river and we swam with ten women, who emerged from the fog dancing, then playing their instruments. These dog walkers walked past. We invited them in, but I think we spooked them.

MUSIC TO SWIM BY

LINDSEY, adventurer and mermaid, ever travelling

I was staying with this woman, Kimmy, and I said, "What's that on your stairs, Kimmy?" She said, "That's my native Indian flute, Lindsey." Then she told me this story about how she accidentally bought three of them when she went to a festival and asked if I wanted her to play it on

BOWLED OVER BY THE SEA

SALLY, community musician, Edinburgh

My best swim was in Tyninghame bay. My best friend, her brother and I stripped and bailed into the sea completely on a whim – the waves were massive and kept bowling us over – it was exhilarating! The water was so clear and beautiful, it made me feel so lucky to live in Scotland and experience her sea!

diverse range of folk, in such a diverse range of places has opened my eyes in more ways than I can think about. I have swum lochs, lakes, waterfalls and reservoirs, played in big surf and snorkelled in some scenic gullies. I have swum in plunge pools wearing my swimming attire on my head and performed handstands with my swimming chums for our amusement and the delight of tourists and bystanders. The merriment drawn by synchro swimming is amazing, as is the breaking of thick ice in February to take a dip in a reservoir. The slightly naughty feeling of walking past the "no swimming" sign to get in the water and the totally liberating feeling of skinny-dipping all add to the fun.

OUT TO PLAY

CHRISTINE, professor of law, Edinburgh

When people ask me when I started wild swimming, I sometimes say a couple of years ago, but the real answer is I've done it all my life. I've always swum. We lived in Derry, and as a child I spent all my summers in Donegal – right up on the most northerly point of Ireland. Because of the conflict, it was quite a magical place for me. We went swimming and I found I could go later and later in the year. I found that there were often really big waves at the equinox in October, which was our half-term break, and that the sea was really quite warm.

I have six children and a job that is very full on. I'm a Professor of Constitutional Law, and a lot of my work involves conflict and post-conflict situations. At the minute I run a big research programme which involves five different

PURE MERRIMENT

RICHARD, security, Edinburgh

I'm not a competitive person, never have been and never will be. I've never been into footy, rugby or team sports. I was a late learner when it came to swimming; swimming lessons in a rock pool at a local beach from my dad were memorable for all the wrong reasons. But I took up scuba-diving in 2004 and dived for about twelve years around the east coast of Scotland. When I found lugging all the kit around and the pre-dive faff a chore, I knocked it on the head in favour of wild swimming.

I joined the Wild Ones of Portobello in 2016, and I've never looked back. To swim with such a

"It's all about having a laugh. For me it's the social-ness, having a laugh, having a bit of fun, going for coffee afterwards. I'm also about endurance and adventure, but only when it's fun. If I'm not enjoying it, there's no point."

CAROLYN, retired doctor, Edinburgh

organisations. We look at how countries use the peace process to address issues of equality and inclusion. It's a career that has partly come out of the fact that I did a lot of human rights activism in the end days of the peace process in Northern Ireland.

My life is a bit impossible. I can't really take off into the mountains that easily – I can, but it needs a lot of planning and for the stars to align on the family front. But I can get down to the water here, and somehow if you go into the water you are in the wild. It's also very social going in with people.

For me, it probably relates to that sensation of childhood. We don't play enough as adults. I've often thought, why not? If we want to get fit, we go to gyms and go on treadmills which historically were torture instruments, and

afterwards you feel virtuous. But I was always fit and healthy as a child because I went out and played. I also liked team sports and doing something collectively, but that's hard to do with my job and my family. I can't hold down a regular commitment, but because you can arrange to swim an hour before and then be with people, it works for me. I like the spontaneity.

Play is important. I see myself as quite serious; I'm quite driven and intense about my work. But having said that, humour is vital to me. I do try to have fun, even with our research team. It was a coping mechanism growing up: there was a very dark sort of humour around the Troubles. Banter and craic and humour are part of the culture of Ireland and Northern Ireland, and that's the case for me too. Swimming taps into a desire for adventure and playfulness.

ALL DRESSED UP

HELEN, management consultant, Scottish Borders

I wore a crab hat for the Scottish Winter Swimming Championships. The crab hat was my first silly hat for wild swimming, but I had form. I used to walk marathons dressed in decorated, themed bras – not at night but in broad daylight in real running marathons. I've been a cowgirl and Tinkerbell. I even had a Chanel tweed one for the Paris marathon. I welcome any opportunity to dress up and add some frivolity. I wear a silly hat because I'm having fun, properly playful daft fun, and a hat feels like an expression of that.

SKINNY-DIPPING INTO PENSIONHOOD

LESLEY, artist, East Lothian

On my sixty-fifth birthday I went on a swim, wearing a necklace I made from the bead-making kit bequeathed to me by my friend Janet, who passed away from cancer. I thought, "Janet never made it to sixty and I'd made it to sixty-five and I want to mark that in some way." It's not written in stone that you become a pensioner at sixty-five, but it is a symbolic year. It was one of my favourite swims of all time. We went down to Yellowcraig and there was nobody around thankfully apart from one man and a dog. It was 23rd January, so it was quite cold but it was beautiful. I whipped off my Dryrobe and it was the best skinny-dip. It was just fabulous. I never would have thought that me as a 65-year-old would have done that. It was just wonderful.

BREAKING THE RULES

NIAMH, carer, East Lothian

Swimming pools can be very difficult when you're autistic, as I am. There are a lot of social rules in swimming pools. You always feel like you might be doing the wrong thing. Other people are so annoying in swimming pools as well. I hate lanes. I hate swimming up and down in lines. I like to swim round and about, and I'm quite childish. I like playing. In the cold-water swimming community, we're generally very accepting of whatever people want to do. I actually think there are a lot of undiagnosed autistic people who are within the cold-water

swimming community. Playing in the water is a really acceptable thing – and I think there is something very childlike about me. There are just not enough opportunities for adults to play.

NIGHT-TIME TRANSGRESSIONS

ANNE, GIS Analyst, Edinburgh

Possibly my most breathlessly gleeful swim was my first night swim, at Portobello beach with some new swimming friends. I'd not been swimming in the dark before and the combination of the cold, the inky water and the slightly transgressive vibe made it absolutely wonderful. Much laughing and gazing up at the starry sky.

REBOOTING THE SYSTEM

GEORGIE, reflexologist, Edinburgh

For me, wild swimming is a complete escape, and a reboot of my whole system. I'm a single mum to a twelve- and thirteen-year-old and feel a great weight of responsibility about their health and wellbeing, education, our financial security, etc. My work can also be quite heavy. I specialise in fertility, so I work with people who are experiencing difficulties conceiving, miscarriages, baby loss, and other health conditions such as endometriosis and menopause. Some days are tough. Getting into cold water and experiencing that initial shock gives me a huge boost and fills me with joy. I love that no two days in the sea are the same, and swimming for a reasonable distance in a flat sea or splashing about in big waves definitely makes life feel less serious and more playful!

SHEER PLEASURE

EMMA, mother, Edinburgh

I swam in a storm on a Sunday morning with forty other Wild Ones. Enormous waves, and even bigger smiles from forty adults playing in the waves. We were jumping and shrieking in pleasure.

"All the girls in my family are wild swimmers.
Me, my daughter Poppy and our dog Ember."

VARI, hotel strategist, Edinburgh

11

FINDING YOUR POD

THE JOY OF THE SWIM COMMUNITY

SWIMMING IN FRIENDSHIP

Alice Goodridge says she is all about the pod. By that she means the people she swims with, the dry-robed imps who hang out with her on the freezing shores of a loch, taking a turn on her ice-cracking sledgehammer, or sharing a cocoa and cake afterwards. It's this desire for a pod, for the fun and company it offers, that led her to set up a swimming group in the Cairngorms, and more recently to organise the Scottish Winter Swimming Championships – an event whose chief purpose, she says, is less about competition and more about "getting together and having fun".

Alice often describes her wild swim adventures as "epic" – but it's clear she thinks that what is still more epic is doing them with someone else.

When we look at the many reasons why swimming may be good for us, the pod is a key factor. Some swimmers are lone fish, and very happy with that, but many say what they love best is swimming with others – sharing the experience, communing. It's the friendships formed; the support networks nurtured. It's the fact that at times when you're lonely, anxious, depressed or struggling, these groups are there, and they aren't socially demanding in the way a visit to a pub might be – you don't have to do a lot of small talk.

A dip with others has almost an instant bonding effect. And with more and more groups popping up on social media, it's getting easier for people to find and connect with that pod almost anywhere they go.

Alice was a fan of the pod from the very first charity swim she did, between islands in the Mediterranean, a challenge which at one point she considered she might not manage because of her fear of extreme water depths. But, she recalls, what helped her was that: "I was surrounded by these other people. I kept myself in the middle of the pod. I felt like, *Nothing will get me if I'm in the middle*. I realised because of that, that I liked being part of the pod. It's all about being part of the pod."

CONNECTIVITY

We humans are social beings, wired to connect. Studies have shown strong correlations between loneliness and social isolation with poor mental and physical health. Social groups like those involved in wild swimming create the kind of connections we all need, and within the context of doing something else that is enormously good for our mental and physical health – exercise.

Many studies now show that exercising in a social group is better for us, in general, than lone exercise. One, published in *The Journal of the American Osteopathic Association* in 2017, found that those working out in a group experience more improvements in lowered stress and quality of life than those working out individually. Its lead researcher, Dayna Yorks, observed, "The communal benefits of coming together with friends and colleagues, and doing something difficult, while encouraging one another, pays dividends beyond exercising alone."

Of course, group swimming isn't the only way to do this. You can go on a ParkRun, join a regular yoga class or cycling club. All these provide many of the same benefits. But many cite that slight element of danger involved in getting in the water as creating an extra sense of mutual support.

"Swimming in itself is quite a vulnerable thing to do," says Stacey. "You're taking most of your clothes off for a start. You're often somewhere very public. Then you're getting into cold water, which is something where you really have to know your own body. It's risky. We've always got to be looking out for each other."

There is something life-affirming about connecting with people in the water. There are swimmers out there who say they have social anxiety and can think of nothing more hellish than a big party – but here, in the water, they find a space of connection. They will describe what goes on there as "instant friendship".

NO BARRIERS IN THE SEA

In the sea, barriers of difference seem to drop. As Anne puts it, "If you're having a moment when you've lost your faith in humanity, go and get in the sea with a lot of people who want to be there. It doesn't matter if your politics don't agree, or if you're having a bad time, everyone is doing the same thing and everyone is enjoying it and you can reset some of your cynicism a bit."

Web developer Chris describes the "community aspect" of his local group, part of Edinburgh's Wild Ones, as vital. "Yes, the connection with nature is really important, but what matters is the connection with other people. It sort of gets down to a basic level. It gets rid of a lot of stuff. We're doing something together that's a bit extreme in a way."

THE OBAN SEALS

Husband and wife Max and Stacey are particularly keen on swimming with the pod. On relocating to Oban in 2018, they decided, after hunting around for and connecting with fellow swimmers, to set up a Facebook group, the Oban Seals, for swimmers to arrange local meet-ups with.

Stacey and Max are, they declare, opposite personalities, one an extrovert and the other an introvert, yet this couple like to do many of the same things together, and that includes going out for a swim with their new-found mates. Max describes Stacey as a "massively social creature" – an assessment with which she agrees. "I like," she says, "bringing people together, but at the same time I don't want to be in charge. I want it to evolve and be its own self-sustaining

thing. I quite like starting things and stepping away and seeing it grow . . ."

She recalls that she didn't actually enjoy outdoor swimming to begin with. Initially she only experimented with it because Max was entering a swimming race and she thought, rather than hang around, she might as well join in. On the first occasion, at the Henley Classic Swim, the race began at 4 a.m. and she suffered. "It was dark and cold and you couldn't see anything in the water. It took me over an hour and I hated it. I just felt: *I can't hear, I can't see and I'm not having fun.*"

It was only when she moved to London and started seeing social media images of adventure groups with "women doing head-up breast-stroke in their cossies, and swimming in the winter" that she realised there was a community out there she might want to be part of.

Swimming as part of a group is still essential to her. "I like doing things with a group,"

she says. "If everyone's doing the same thing, you get quite a high from that. Perhaps it's programmed into us, maybe it's why the army make people march? You gain a lot of trust and a sense of community from those who are doing the same thing as you."

A PAIR THAT'S A POD

The social aspect of swimming doesn't have to be about taking the plunge in a large group – it can be about finding a swim buddy who shares your passion and going on an adventure with them. It can be about taking a dip with your kids, or your partner.

Two, in fact, can be a pod. One of the joys of *Taking the Plunge* has been hearing the stories of the many swim buddies who have paired over a shared love of water. Friends, for instance, like Matt and Gordon, who roam Skye looking for new swim spots; one a spritely goat, maned with dreadlocks, the other a sturdy six-foot-four ponytailed bear, who describe each other as "heterosexual life partners".

Or Edinburgh buddies, Cat and Louise, who met at a swim celebrating the shortest day of the year in 2017. "I really have no clue how it happened," Cat says, "but we are now close friends! We just swam and went out together." Some of those swim adventures, on what they called their Edinborders challenge to swim on every beach in East Lothian and the Borders, would be five-dip days, plunging from bay to bay.

It's perhaps not surprising that these tight bonds form. Something special happens when you get in the water with someone. You go on a small journey with them, from cold shock to finding yourself, on the other side, seeing the world a little differently. People frequently talk about being able to offload, too. As Anne puts it, "You can have a good heart-to-heart with someone out in the sea – in the way that you can do in the car when you're both facing forward and there's no one else around."

OUR SWIMMING FAMILY

Many of those who swim to counter pain say the social element is as important to them as the pain relief. Dawn, who has suffered chronic, debilitating pain, talks about her "swim family" and how "the social aspect" has helped her. "You get the buzz from the water, and then the buzz from the people around you is just incredible. As soon as I feel sore now, I think, *Right, I need to get in the water*. But the best part is I also do it with my swimming family."

She recalls the ways in which her swim family and the water helped her on another swim trip, when she was almost unable to move. "They literally took me to the water's edge, changed me into my Dryrobe. I sat in the most amazing water I've ever been in in my entire life. I came out and again I was in pain, but not the level of pain I've been in before. Just that buzz of 'oh my God, I've done this' helps reduce my pain."

For Dawn, as for many people, it's not just about the act of swimming. "It's about," she says, "being with other people, being outside, being so close to nature, just getting out of your house. If you're in the water for two minutes you will feel proud of yourself. Isolation and loneliness have a big impact on depression, and the social aspect of wild swimming really helps."

This doesn't mean the social side of swimming is easy for all, or that everyone bonds with a pod of their own. The people we spoke to are those who found their tribe in swimming – they're bound to rave about it. But there may be others who do not or who enjoy the solitude of swimming alone.

CHILLY DIPPERS

OLIVIA, student, Edinburgh

Before I started swimming, I often found myself a little bit anxious about the future, stressed about small things and generally in a bit of a confusion about how the world works – let alone being at university. I would take time out from my friends and the university workload for some solitude and thinking time often accompanied by a swim. I didn't know at first what it was that made me feel so much better, the adrenaline of getting into the cold water, the juxtaposition of sitting in the library with a heavy head and the lightness of the water, or the feeling of accomplishment from coming out of the freezing waters. All in all, it was a feeling that counterbalanced the stress and anxiety of my life and something I wanted more people to experience. After some extensive research I realised a key theme: the cold water works in reducing stress by promoting endorphins and adrenaline. Swimming's never been terribly cool; this was something I wanted to challenge by making all different types of people dive straight into it.

I started a swim group called Chilly Dippers as a way of reforming the student lifestyle. Instead of meeting around a pub table, drinking away, I thought, "Why not get out, meet new

"I love swimming in the cold sea with my mum. It is so fun, but the best bit is getting all cosy and warm and having hot chocolate afterwards."

FINLAY, age ten

people and have an hour to escape the usual humdrum of student life?" That's really what is so addictive – the feeling of escapism from one's other responsibilities when being fully immersed in the freezing cold water. Needless to say, it's been a great way to meet new people and encourage more people to talk about their own mental health struggles around like-minded people. The meet-ups are busier closer to exam season, when stress levels are significantly higher – perhaps illustrating how cold-water swimming is nature's best de-stresser!

I have watched wild swimming bond everyone together – from first-time dippers to avid cold-water enthusiasts. Those enthusiasts like to help first timers while simultaneously experiencing those first-time endorphin levels rise as they live their experiences vicariously through one another. Wild swimming is by no means a competitive sport, nor does it require any sort of specialised skill to participate. It's an activity where members encourage everyone to see swimming more as a therapeutic exercise both for the mind and body.

CIRCLES OF FRIENDS

SARAH, swimming coach and Pilates teacher, Cairngorms

It's nice having a community. It's probably the first time in my life where I've actually had quite a few friends and you're like *this is amazing*. I'm quite quiet usually. I normally have one or two close friends and I've got quite a big circle now.

FOR A BOB AND A BLETHER

SUE, press officer for Scottish Athletics and Jog Scotland, Edinburgh

I've always loved swimming outdoors. As a kid I swam every summer in the North Sea at Walton-on-the-Naze in Essex, and my parents would have to call me in, shouting, "Susie! Your lips are blue!"

I kept it up sporadically after that – back in the early 2000s I was a journalist in North London and reported on the redoubtable women of the Kenwood Ladies' Pond Association, who at the time were fighting for the right to break the ice on the pond for their traditional Christmas swim. (They won. Of course they won.) I would swim there on my way home from work, but only really in the warmer months.

Then, in 2010, the Outdoor Swimming Society hosted a spring swim in North Berwick. I was then a reporter on the *Edinburgh Evening News* and was sent along to write about it, so I thought I might as well give the swim a go, too.

Afterwards, some of us were stood drinking tea and agreed we'd like to keep in touch and arrange future swims together. After a while of batting emails back and forth, I set up a Facebook group called the Wild Ones as an easier way for us to keep in touch. Gradually, over time, we'd add people we'd met on beaches, or friends who were interested in trying it . . . and now we have 2,100 members!

It's been a tremendous change – there used to be a handful of us swimming, and anyone who saw us drying off after would ask if we were "those nutters that swim in the sea". Now there are scores of people, and nobody bats an eyelid. It's great to see it flourishing – though sometimes you still have to sneak off for a quiet swim away from the crowds.

It's always been an inclusive group, and the great thing is that ethos is still there, even though we've grown nearly 200-fold. It doesn't matter whether you're a triathlete or just go for a bob and a blether – by stepping into the water, you're one of us. Nobody has time for ego when you're all trying to get back into your pants without exposing yourself on the beach.

Many of my best friends now are people I've met through swimming – even if we don't swim together these days, the friendships have stuck. As you meet by the water, there's an instant bond and you leave everything else behind. Whoever you are in the rest of your life, and whatever's happening on shore, once you're in the water, it's the swim that's important.

I'm not a religious person, but when I've been having a regular swim in a regular spot, it's the nearest I've come to going to church. There's a sense you're connected to something bigger than yourself, a feeling of community, and – as you see the water and the world go through the seasons – there's the sense that everything changes, but it all stays the same.

MOTHER AND DAUGHTER

ANGIE, psychotherapist, Edinburgh

My youngest daughter is ten and she always wants to come in the water with me. In those moments I have that extra special connection with my daughter. I'm not just connecting with me and the world and the elements and all this beautiful marine life, which I'm massively grateful for, but I've also got that more intimate connection with my daughter. It's special. You're playing. There's something so joyful in that.

BRAVING THE ELEMENTS

FIONA, retired social worker, Cairngorms

I went along to a wild-swim taster session on exposed Lochindorb, in strong winds and bitter cold. Alice Goodridge led the swim, which was an amazingly exhilarating experience – out to the island and back. It was freezing and I noticed the experienced swimmers had Dryrobes. I felt envy! In order to justify such an acquisition, I joined Cairngorm Wild Swimmers who swim

at Loch Morlich on a Sunday, all year round. I loved the swim but was hooked by the feeling of camaraderie as we all braved the elements. By the time we had a post-swim coffee I really felt I had found my tribe.

A PROFOUND KIND OF KNOWING

SUSIE, occupational therapist, Edinburgh

There are various things in my life that I do with people – in which it's not like I know all about them or they know all about me. We might not know, for instance, what each other does for a job or not a job. We know each other in a different way. There's something very nice about the fact that you know that person for that minute in that different and sometimes quite profound way. When you're bobbing about in the freezing cold in the water, you can have really profound conversations. It's not that you do anything about what's said, or feel that you must meet for coffee after, or anything. You find out the most extraordinary things about people, that you haven't asked, but it all just sort of flows out with the water and hangs there. It floats.

COMING HOME TOGETHER

Not everyone manages to bond with a pod of their own, nor does everyone want to. There's nothing wrong – except it's a little more dangerous – with a lone swim. But we have certainly observed that, for many, a huge part of the buzz is the company. It's the support network. It's

the shared experience. It's those extraordinary conversations that Susie speaks of. It's knowing each other in a different way. It's the feeling that someone else gets something about you because they get that same bonkers thrill in the waves.

But also, it's as if that almost existential sense of belonging that people get in the water is taken to an extra level by swimming together. Niamh, who is autistic and swims with others in the Wild Ones, expresses this particularly well. Her body, she says, feels "more right" when she swims. "When I'm in the water, I feel so much more like I'm biologically supposed to and I feel like I've come home when I'm in there. And when I swim with a big group, when I go out with the local group, which I don't do very often, I have this amazing sense that I'm part of a pod of animals."

"Swimming is not nearly so good when there's no one there to share it with. You know the way that if there's a film that you really love you want to show it to your friends so you can see their reaction. It's a little like that. You need your joy to be reflected a bit."
ANNE, Edinburgh

12

STAYING
SAFE

HEALTH AND SAFETY
IN THE WATER

This chapter is absolutely essential to keep you safe, well informed and up to speed with how to be a wild swimmer with the savvy and self-awareness to be responsible for yourself and others.

THE ART OF SEA SWIMMING

COLIN CAMPBELL, swim coach

Swimming kit

The only thing you need to go swimming is yourself. A costume is a good idea so as not to scare the local wildlife, and some goggles so you can see the murk below better, and a bright-coloured cap to keep your head warm . . . and to make you more visible (I prefer silicon to latex). But apart from that, everything else is about after your swim.

After-swim kit

Start with a towel. You want something big enough to wrap round you and change under. Some people go for the micro-fleece beach towels, but I'm not a fan. My wife prefers a poncho-type towel (Dryrobe is the main brand) to change under.

You also want loose, warm clothes to quickly and easily put on as soon as you're dry, starting with a T-shirt or two. Choose clothes you can chuck on without any faff; your fingers might be numb, you might have the judders, and your skin might be all sticky because it's cold and fresh out of the water. After a swim I often put on two T-shirts, a baggy base layer, a jumper, a thick shirt, and a hoodie. Thick socks (loose!) are also recommended. And a hat. Do not forget the hat! Warm and woolly (or fleecy), obviously.

It can be a good idea to have your clothes handy and laid out before you go in the water. The trick is to get dressed as quick as you can so you can get moving to help your body warm up again. Your core temperature will drop a degree or three once you're out of the water as the cold layer of blood below your skin is recirculated around your body, causing a condition called after drop, which some people call the judders, and the medical term for which is peripheral vasoconstriction.

Another useful bit of kit is something to stand on, whether that's flip-flops, Crocs, or a square of a foam sleeping mat or yoga mat. This keeps your feet off the cold or wet ground and stops the heat seeping out from under you.

And finally, take a flask containing a hot drink. It's a superb way to warm up afterwards; just be careful if you're shaking from the judders.

Getting in

Of course, it's the actual getting in that can be the hardest thing – both mentally and physically – but there are ways to make it easier for yourself.

I prefer to dive or jump in for that exhilarating cold-water blast, but it's not for everybody, and probably not for cold-water newbies. Walking in is the safer option, though it's murder on your soles if it's across pebbles or rocks. (Swim socks are often a good idea.)

If you do walk in, those first few seconds around your ankles can be a wee bit nippy. You'll wonder how you can keep going and want to claw back out. But keep going! It gets easier, and once your calves, knees, thighs are in things start settling down. Maybe stop, pause,

count to twenty, and continue past your waist.

Another important tip is to get your hands in as soon as possible. Use them to splash some water on your chest, on your back and neck, and on your face as you're walking in. This distracts from the water around your legs or abdomen, but it also prepares you physiologically for going in, reducing the effects of cold-water shock!

Cold-water shock

The thing that happens when you gasp for breath and your muscles contract is called cold-water shock. It can make people panicky, but it's also quite exciting. Your adrenaline is kicking in. Let your body settle into the cold by rolling on to your back. Kick your legs hard. Scull for a bit. Swear, shout, shriek if it helps; you won't be the first! As your body and mind calm, focus on

your exhalations, and then remind yourself how unbelievable lucky (and brave) you are to be in this gorgeous sea, loch, or river.

Getting the face in

Once you're happy enough in the water it's time to get your face in and start swimming. For me, that's the hardest part especially when the water's really cold. The swimming cap helps a lot here. And wearing two will make a massive difference. You need a cap for visibility, but also because it reduces the brain freeze. Pull it down over your ears and down over your forehead to just above your eyes.

If getting your face in is a struggle, try the following water polo drill: dip your head in during every other stroke, ensuring you exhale fully to maintain control of your breathing. Another strategy is to submerge your whole

able to breathe when and where you want, but you'll likely be faced with swims where you have to be able to breathe on only the right or left sides. Like your freestyle stroke itself, the key is being able to adapt. Also, without lane ropes or markers to guide you, you may veer in one direction: bilateral breathing helps reduce this.

Swimming direct into the chop can be quite challenging – and immensely fun – but it's sometimes tricky to avoid getting a face full of water. Try to pierce each wave, rather than fight over them. If you're side on to the waves, just try to roll with it. Enjoy the sensation! But be mindful of how it can affect where you're going.

Sighting

Again, if you're swimming front crawl, it's vital that you practise and have an awareness of how to sight. Ultimately, we all swim at our own risk, and that means responsibility for your own safety is always on you, and that includes navigation. There are no lane ropes in the wild and distance can be surprisingly tricky to judge, so use landmarks to help you. Tall trees, church spires, mountains, buoys, brightly coloured buildings, and so on. Always know which direction you're swimming in.

As for sighting technique, one common way is to lift your eyes just above the water immediately before taking a breath, and then rotate your head as you take a breath as part of the same movement. Another method is to lift your head as your arm goes into the water and stretches out in front of you. Do this regularly (perhaps every fourth or fifth breath), and always have an awareness of how the water flow is directing you.

head a few times, especially the back of your head and neck. This balances out the coldness front and back and helps you acclimatise. It can be painful initially, but the more you do it, the easier it gets.

Cold-water swimming

Water conditions vary like the weather, and wind, current and tide will all affect the water, which will obviously impact your stroke.

If you enjoy freestyle – though it's by no means compulsory – it's a good idea to practise different techniques when in the pool. Short strokes with a high recovery and an early entry for when it's very choppy and the swell is lifting you up and down. Or longer stokes and extended glides for when the water's calm.

If you're swimming freestyle, bilateral breathing is an important skill. Most times you'll be

COLD-WATER SHOCK RESPONSE: THE SCIENCE

DR CLARE EGLIN, expert in cold-water response, the University of Portsmouth

Most people who fall in cold water don't die from hypothermia, nor do they simply drown. What kills them is cold-water shock response. Here Dr Clare Eglin explains what it is and how to deal with it.

What is cold-water shock response?

What we call cold-water shock response is caused by rapid cooling of the skin usually due to going into cold water. This stimulates receptors in the skin which then activates the sympathetic nervous system – the fight or flight system. The response is an inspiratory gasp following by uncontrollable hyperventilation (breathing very fast), increased heart rate and blood pressure.

For young, healthy individuals, the lack of control over breathing is the main problem as it can induce panic, interferes with swimming and increases the chances of aspirating water and therefore drowning. In individuals who have underlying cardiovascular disease, the increased workload of the heart could also cause a heart attack. If possible, wait until the cold shock response has subsided before you go out of your depth and / or start swimming.

How can I adapt?

The response is caused by rapid cooling of the skin, so if you can reduce this you will reduce the response. The response is probably at its greatest at water temperature of 15°C, so going in warmer water will result in a lesser response.

Wearing a wetsuit or a drysuit will also reduce the response. The cold shock response lasts about three minutes with the maximum response occurring within a minute. Therefore, if you go in slowly, gradually exposing the skin to the cold water, the response will be reduced. In addition, with repeated immersions in cold water (or practice with cold showers) the response will be reduced – this process of habituation can last many months. Individuals with greater body fat are not protected from the response, though they may find it easier to float.

Am I healthy enough to swim?

As with any new exercise, it may be advisable to check with your GP that the activity is safe for you to do. For example, when we are undertaking cold-water immersions for our research, we exclude people who are not accustomed to maximal exercise, have a history of cardiovascular disease or have asthma and, if we are using very cold water, then all participants will have a medical.

SAFETY TIPS FOR WATERFALLS, RESERVOIRS, QUARRIES AND RIVERS

SARAH WISEMAN, swim coach

1. Waterfalls

Waterfalls are great fun, aren't they? Or are they? Here are three things to be aware of when swimming in or around waterfalls:

- The height of the waterfall will affect the strength of it.
- The flow rate of the waterfall: its power is affected by the rate of the flow.
- No matter how the waterfall has been or looked before, judge the waterfall in the present moment.

2. Reservoirs

Reservoirs come with some risk factors that are obvious and some that are less so. Always check out the signage around the reservoir and follow any guidance stated. Entry and exit points apply just the same as for other swims. Pick a spot wisely. Here are some things to think about:

- Steep sides / banks.
- Sudden changes in the depth of water.
- Hidden machinery – whether on land or in the water.
- Underwater currents.
- Reservoir dams and towers; towers are usually close to the dam.
- Spillways on the dam.
- Dam overflows.
- Underwater pipes.
- Be aware if you are swimming downstream of a reservoir.
- Aerators (usually marked with buoys), and any sudden loss of buoyancy near an aerator.
- Check the legality of swimming in a reservoir (some permit swimming; a lot don't).

3. Quarries

Quarries can vary greatly in size, depth and accessibility. Look out for the following if you take a swim in a quarry:

- Steep sides / banks.
- Sudden changes in the depth of water.
- Underwater hazards.
- Temperature changes (quarries tend to be like lakes in how they behave temperature-wise).
- Currents / flow from the filler streams.
- Pollution (check what was quarried there).
- Check the legality of swimming in a quarry (there are issues around right of access, right to roam etc).

4. Rivers

Rivers can offer joyful, fast-flowing and expansive swim experiences, or quieter, more intimate ones. Every river is different, but please be aware of the following:

- Siphons: These are caused by a gap between rocks, causing water to be forced through (rather like a plug being removed). From a swimmer's point, you can be sucked towards the gap and pinned (like a plug being put in). This makes it extremely hard to move and get out of.
- Sieve: This is caused by fallen trees or overhanging roots; swimmers can find themselves pushed against roots or the bank. The strength of the water will hold a swimmer there and they will struggle to get out or away.
- Flash Rivers: conditions in a flash river will change very quickly especially with additional rainfall.

- High banks of a river: this can make it very difficult to get out, they could be covered in moss, and wet or damp soil.
- Rivers may be colder than expected.
- That favourite jumping spot can become unsafe due to fluctuation in the depth of the river.
- Be aware of natural stoppers and learn how to spot them.

Wherever you choose to swim, please stay safe and be sensible – the water will always be there for you, so if anything seems at all risky it's better to stay on the shore and swim another day!

PARTING WORDS

SHARING THE PLUNGE

I remember when Anna first showed me her swimming photos. I was captivated by the look on people's faces. The goofy grimace, the crazed grin, the gasp of surprise. Those expressions told a story. Those swimmers were throwing caution to the wind and waves. I recognised something in those faces – something I had felt at times myself. The elation that follows getting over some sense of fear or reluctance. The pleasure to be found in simply taking the plunge.

There is, of course, more than one way to take the plunge. You don't have to throw yourself into an ice-covered lake or dive into a gushing waterfall to test yourself. There are other ways of flinging caution aside. But we hope we've made here a strong case for the thrills, pleasures and health benefits to be gained by plunging into one of nature's pools, with a kick and a splash.

We aren't claiming that wild swimming is the solution to all health problems. There were times, on our swim travels, when I joked that our dips were doing the opposite. I had a sore neck. The whole project was stressing me out. Was it having a weird effect on my hips? But then there would be one of those amazing, atmospheric swims. In the silvery dusk of midsummer, watching bubbles flutter like diamonds through the darkness, arms like ghosts parting the water ahead. There would be a calm that followed. There would be a sense that world-worries – about the climate and global politics – were put in perspective at least for a moment.

By the way, I don't think it's a coincidence that wild swimming has seen such a boom at a time when there is such intense, widespread anxiety about the environment. There is, I suspect, a connection.

But the story told here – the stories others told us – is mostly about the physical benefits of wild swimming. Scientists are just beginning to research the therapeutic effects of cold water. Why it makes us feel so good, why it eases pain or alleviates depression needs more probing. But we have little doubt that it does help. Swimmers told us this again and again. We, as swimmers, already know it ourselves.

Beyond physiological benefits, there is something else. Cold-water swimming teaches us about living. It's there in the title of this book. Fear can leave us standing too often on the shoreline. We can teeter too long, let our worries inflate.

The people we swam with in the creation of *Taking the Plunge* took us to places we might otherwise not have gone. They seemed accustomed to life outside the comfort zone. Matt Rhodes coached us into the depths of a tiny cave where a waterfall hammered torrents over our heads. A Channel swimmer took us off on a breaststroke saunter in a loch that stretched on for ever.

We even braved baring all in a mass skinny dip. Early in the morning on a city beach, as a huge cruise liner passed, we took a dip with thirty naked people – or thirty almost naked people. A few were still wearing neoprene swim socks. One sported a floral bathing hat.

As we travelled the country, we were paddling in the wake of swimmers far more daring than ourselves – Alice Goodridge, Calum Maclean, Gilly McArthur, Lindsey Cole, Kate Swaine, Max Holloway, Sandra Lea. But we were also swimming in the metaphorical wash of glorious heroes like *Waterlog* pioneer Roger Deakin, endurance athlete Lynne Cox, round-Britain legend Ross Edgley or marathon swimmer Beth French.

We went places we never dreamed
we would. You could too. Perhaps you
already have. We have been so inspired
and hope you have been too.

We'd love to hear and see news of your
wild swimming adventures! Please share
with us at #mywildswim.

OUR TOP 10 PLACES TO SWIM IN SCOTLAND

1. **Loch Insh, Cairngorms.** A glorious sunset spot, surrounded by woodlands. The Boathouse restaurant serves hearty food and is perfect for warming up in afterwards.

2. **Loch Morlich, Rothiemurcus.** Where the Cairngorm Wild Swimmers meet every Sunday, this loch has the virtue of having a proper sandy beach.

3. **Portobello Beach, Edinburgh.** The key dipping spot for Edinburgh's Wild Ones and a great place to start. It's a good idea to swim parallel to the beach, between the groynes.

4. **Pittenweem tidal swimming pool, Fife.** Swim old-style, as it always used to be done in the many tidal pools that were once

dotted along our coastlines. Plans are afoot for its restoration – hurrah! Follow your dip with hot chocolate at the Cocoa Tree café.

5. **Loch Lubnaig, Callendar.** Beautiful, and the first loch you hit as you head north into the Trossachs. It's nestled between Ben Ledi, Benvane and Ben Vorlich. Watch out – there's a ledge as you walk in, then a sharp drop off into deep water. Park at the Forestry Commission car park with the café and get a warming coffee afterwards.

6. **Camusdarach beach.** Gorgeous white sands, rocky outcrops and pools, plus incredible views out towards Eigg. We like to do this swim from a stay at the Camusdarach campsite.

7. **Seacliff beach, East Lothian.** A private beach, which charges for parking, but with stunning views of Tantallon and the Bass Rock.

8. **River Feshie at Feshiebridge.** There's an easy get-in to the river here, from a stop-off on the B970, and if you swim a little upstream you'll come into a large river pool, formed as the river narrows towards the bridge.

9. **Loch Tay, Taymouth Marina.** The only loch in Scotland where you can follow a dip in the chilly waters with a warming session in a sauna, the Hot Box, afterwards.

10. **Loch Voil, Balquhidder.** Reached by a tiny road, along the north side of the loch, you can enjoy a wonderful dip at the meeting point between Loch Doine and Loch Voil. Tuck into soup and sandwiches at Monachyle Mhor afterwards.

ALL YOU'LL EVER NEED

1. A swimsuit

Our best advice is to start in the summer when the water's at its warmest. For your first swim all you really need is your swimsuit and a smile. And, to be honest, the swimsuit is non-essential!

2. Socks

If you are going to invest a little, then neoprene socks are great. We tend to wear them all year round; they protect your feet against anything sharp and take the edge off the cold. They range in thickness, so you may want to try a few options. We love the 5mm socks for winter swims.

3. Gloves

We also like neoprene gloves for colder water swimming. Again, the thickness varies and for winter swimming we go for the 3mm or 5mm. It's always your hands and feet that feel the cold the most, so we recommend these neoprene extras over wetsuits.

4. A hat

Many people advise a bright swimming hat so you are visable in the water. They also do a great job at keeping your head insulated. You can buy a neoprene cap, which is brilliant for preventing ice-cream head in the colder months. We often pop on a bobble hat to keep our heads nice and cosy during a swim.

5. A wetsuit

A swimming wetsuit is fabulous, but it's an expensive option, so start simple and add, rather than going all out and investing immediately in a wetsuit. Again, they vary in thickness, and type. There are plenty of proper swim wetsuits, which are much better for front crawl and more flexible than traditional wet or dry suits made for water sports.

A wetsuit means you can stay in the water much longer, but they can be a faff. They also increase your buoyancy, perfect if you are distance swimming, especially in the winter.

6. Floats

Many people use a tow float to carry essentials (keys, phone, etc), but also as a buoyancy aid on longer swims. They are usually brightly coloured in order to be visible to boats.

7. Other paraphernalia

- Goggles are great, especially if you like to swim crawl. And the serious among us might invest in prescription goggles if our eyes might thank us for them.
- A big warm towel – or a Dryrobe – is ideal for post-swim drying and warmth.
- An old towel or square of yoga or camping mat to stand on while you change.
- Swimmers often like those swim-kit string bags for putting wet stuff in afterwards.
- A flask or sturdy water bottle – for rehydrating with hot and cold drinks.
- Snacks – swimming can be hungry work!
- All these things can be adjusted, upgraded, begged, borrowed and shared as you embark on your swimming journey. One of the joys of wild swimming is its lo-fi philosophy. Fancy, expensive or abundant kit is not required on your wild swim adventure!

THANK YOU

Thank you from us both

Thanks to the amazing catalyst that is Gill Scott, who introduced us, and even suggested we might like to do a book together. We owe you all the crazy fun and friendship that followed.

To Jenny Brown, our agent, for believing in us, and to all at Black & White – Ali, Campbell, Emma, Jaz, Thomas, Tonje – for making this the book we dreamed of.

Most of all, a huge thanks to the incredible people we swam with – including the Edinburgh Wild Ones, the Cairngorm Wild Swimmers, the Oban Seals, Calum Maclean, Matt from @soakupskye. This book is yours. You are its heart and inspiration. Thanks for being involved, for sharing yourselves with us and swimming alongside us.

Thank you from Anna

It's hard to believe my photography project is now an actual book! I have so many people to thank for helping this dream become a reality.

Vicky, my writing partner and dear swim friend, thank you for taking this journey with me. Lil, for being my swimming partner, my inspiration and motivation to get in the water in the first place.

To my parents, Addy and Helen, for your support, love and encouragement in everything I do. Lizzie, for helping me find my wild and being the best sister a girl could ask for. My brother Jamie for your friendship and great advice. My Granny Pat, I always looked for the bird in every frame; you inspired my photography, thank you always for that. My dear Grandma Sylvia, whose love of the sea, beautiful art and tales of Shetland inspire me so much.

Aunty Mary, my third granny, always lovely to chat and drink tea with you. I love you three so very dearly.

To my Wardie Bay Swim Friends, thank you for all the swims in all weathers, this journey wouldn't have started without you guys.

My Local Lassies, Nic M, Nic B, Katie, Jenny, Ali, Diane and Dixie, also Tracy, Lucy, Jenny, Betty, Claire, my cousin Mairi, thank you for being my girls . . . your support through this and so much else means the world to me.

Finally, to my patient, loving and gorgeous husband Rob and my wonderful, wild, brilliant children Lily and Finlay. Thank you for understanding when work took me away, for celebrating with me, for cuddles when I was cold, for cheerleading from the shore and for being the best family I could wish for. I love you.

Thank you from Vicky

An ocean of thanks to those I love most – my husband Andy and sons Louis and Max, who have swum with me, but have also put up with the long weekends when Mum was "off swimming". Some of my favourite dips have still been with you.

Thanks to Mum and Dad, Sylvia and Stuart, for the early beach memories and a lifetime of the kind of "take the plunge" encouragement that makes me feel I can give most things a try.

To Bryony for thinking of me when you wanted to start dipping at Porty, and Lynn and Carolyn for making it such a laugh. But most of all, my biggest thanks, to Anna – you are, literally, the vision. You've been such a wonderful, inspiring companion. What a way to get to know each other.

ABOUT THE AUTHORS

ANNA DEACON has worked as a photographer for over a decade following a career in the music industry in London. Her photographic work has been published in *The Times*, *The Scotsman*, *The Herald*, *Hood*, *The Big Issue*, *Refinery 29*, *Sunday Post* and *Outdoor Swimmer*, and many others. She loves to photograph the great outdoors and enjoys portrait and documentary work. Anna has organised community swims, beach cleans, and fundraising for mental health charities within the swimming community.

VICKY ALLAN is an award-winning journalist and author. A staff writer for the *Herald on Sunday*, her work has also appeared in *The Times*, *Daily Express*, *Vogue*, *GQ*, the *Guardian* and *Scotland on Sunday*. She has won awards for her travel writing, features writing and for her articles campaigning against violence against women. Her novel *Stray* is currently being adapted as a feature film. She has always loved the outdoors and wild places.

HERE'S TO THE POD!

You've been epic.
Thanks for all the swims.

BE INSPIRED

Further reading

Stuart Brown, *Play: How It Shapes the Brain, Opens the Imagination, and Invigorates the Soul*, Penguin Putnam (2010)

Scott Carney, *What Doesn't Kill Us: how freezing water, extreme altitude, and environmental conditioning will renew our lost evolutionary strength*, Scribe (2019)

Lynne Cox, *Swimming to Antarctica: Tales of a Long-distance Swimmer*, Phoenix (2016)

Lynne Cox, *Open Water Swimming Manual: An Expert's Survival Guide for Triathletes and Open Water Swimmers*, Vintage (2013)

Mihaly Csikszentmihalyi, *Flow: The Psychology of Optimal Experience*, Rider (2002)

Roger Deakin, *Waterlog: A Swimmer's Journey Through Britain*, Chatto & Windus (1999)

Ruth Fitzmaurice, *I Found My Tribe, Vintage (2018)*

Tristan Gooley, How To Read Water: Clues & Patterns from Puddles to the Sea, *Sceptre (2017)*

Alexandra Heminsley, *Leap In: A Woman, Some Waves, and the Will to Swim*, Hutchinson (2017)

Alastair Humphreys, *Microadventures: Local Discoveries for Great Escapes*, William Collins (2014)

Jack Hudson, *Swim Wild: Dive into the natural world and discover your inner adventure*, Yellow Kite (2018)

Amy Liptrot, *The Outrun*, Canongate (2018)

Joe Minihane, *Floating: A Life Regained*, Abrams Press (2017)

Alanna Mitchell, *Sea Sick: The Global Ocean In Crisis*, McClelland & Stewart (2009)

Wallace J. Nichols, *Blue Mind: How Water Makes You Happier, More Connected and Better at What You Do*, Abacus (2018)

Kate Rew, *Wild Swim*, Random House (2008)

Daniel Start, *Wild Swimming: 300 Hidden Dips in the Rivers, Lakes and Waterfalls of Britain*, Wild Things Publishing (2013, revised edition)

Tessa Wardley, *The Mindful Art of Wild Swimming*, Leaping Hare Press (2017)

Victoria Whitworth, *Swimming With Seals*, Head of Zeus (2017)

Journals & Studies

Qing Li, 'Effect of forest bathing on human immune function', *Environmental Health and Preventive Medicine*, January 2010; 15(1)

Tipton M., et al, 'Cold water immersion: kill or cure?', *Experimental Physiology*, 102.11, 2017

Tom B. Mole, Pieter Mackeith, 'Cold forced open-water swimming: a natural intervention to improve postoperative pain and mobilisation outcomes?', *BMJ Case Reports*, 2018

Otto Muzik, Kaice T. Reill, Vaibhav A. Diwadkard, '"Brain over body" – A study on the willful regulation of autonomic function during cold exposure', *Neuroimage*, 2018

Van Tulleken C., Tipton M., Massey H., et al, 'Open water swimming as a treatment for major depressive disorder', *Case Reports*, 2018

Twohig-Bennett & Jones, 'The health benefits of the great outdoors: A systematic review and meta-analysis of greenspace exposure and health outcomes', *Environmental Research*, October 2018; 166

Dayna M. Yorks, Christopher A. Frothingham, Mark D. Schuenke, 'Effects of Group Fitness Classes on Stress and Quality of Life of Medical Students', *The Journal of the American Osteopathic Association*, 2017

Instagram accounts you might like to follow

@wildswimmingstories
@wayoutsideuk
@soakupskye
@caldamac
@ellachloeswims
@chillydippers
@deakinandblue
@tonicofthesea
@wildwelshswimmer
@outdoorswimmingsociety
@beyondthewater_uk
@swimwild_uk